Praise for

YOU CAN'T MAKE T... ... ..

"The lessons learned about employee engagement are spot on, as happy employees make for happy customers. Being a seafarer, this book kept me interested because I could relate to many of the subjects written about. It is light hearted, yet very informative and educational. Having worked with Paul, I wish him well with the successful publishing of this very entertaining book."

—Valerie Contreras
Human Resources Manager

"Educational, entertaining, and fascinating. There is much to take away from *You Can't Make This Ship Up*. From customer service skills to a good laugh, it's a must-read for anyone who finds cruise life intriguing. The best stories are the ones you really can't make up! It is in these wild situations where you learn some of the biggest life lessons and get a front-row seat to just how strange people really can be. Paul ties it all together so beautifully in this book."

—Sarah Dandashy
Travel and Hospitality Expert, Ask A Concierge

"A must read for cruise enthusiasts, as well as any business owner, manager, or supervisor who wants to learn valuable lessons and apply them to their bottom line. Reading Paul's book was like living my ship life again. So many stories of a life that only crew members would understand. Now passengers will get a glimpse of what went on behind the scenes to ensure 'the ship goes on.'"

—Gordon Whatman, Former Cruise Director

"*You Can't Make This Ship Up* is highly educational, hilariously entertaining, and so incredibly true. Reading through it made me laugh, got me super excited, and brought occasional tears to my eyes. I've had the true pleasure of sailing with Paul on numerous cruises and felt privileged to witness his professionalism, the quality of his leadership, and his people skills. I know it came from Paul's heart."

—Captain Marek Slaby
Royal Caribbean International

"Working in the hospitality industry, specifically the cruise line segment, for over thirty years, I have found that it is crucial to work as a 'team' at all times. There will be occasions when a curve ball will be thrown at you, just as there are in all walks of life, and here is when it is so important to use your critical thinking and come up with fast solutions and always remain calm in your presentation and follow-through. Paul's book tells you how to do this in a fun and entertaining way with wonderful stories and great lessons for any business."

—Diana Bloss
CEO and Charter Manager, Worldwide Cruise Associates

"Who knew a business book could be fun, insightful, and useful, all at the same time? Paul Rutter's unique blend of put-you-in-scene stories and pragmatic tips make this a page-turner. As he says, we're all in the same boat, and these innovative insights can help you and your team work together more effectively, come hell or high water."

—Sam Horn
CEO of the Intrigue Agency

"What a terrific book on how to apply Paul's lessons learned from forty-plus years working on a cruise ship to any business. Paul is a fabulous storyteller and writer, and illustrates his wise points with amusing true stories from his cruises. I especially enjoyed his parenthetical comments that made it feel like he was sitting next to me."

—Rebecca Morgan
Bestselling Author, Morgan Seminar Group

"This is a must-read for leaders who want to embody a customer-centric mindset and build every moment around the experience and not just the transaction. As someone who has achieved a Diamond Status on a cruise line, believe Paul Rutter when he says, 'You can't make this SHIP up.' Paul uses witty storytelling of real-life experiences and events to remind us of the value of relationSHIP through leaderSHIP. From my perspective, life is always funnier than fiction."

—Dr. Troy Hall
Global Speaker, Radio Host, Talent Retention Strategist, and Bestselling Author of *Cohesion Culture: Proven Principles to Retain Your Top Talent* and *FANNY RULES: A Mother's Leadership Lessons That Never Grow Old*

"What a journey! *You Can't Make This Ship Up* is a tidal wave of practical business solutions through real-life experiences which are both entertaining and informative. Paul's relatable scenarios in an industry which holds accountability in high regard on a consistent basis proves that his methods get results quickly and effectively."

—Craig Coffey
Television News Anchor, Executive Producer

"If you are looking for a book that can show you how to exceed your customers' expectations, then this is the one. Paul talks about how customer service doesn't end when they are on a ship. It's twenty-four hours a day, and there needs to be a backup plan for everything—even if it's just in case something goes wrong with their travel plans. The ideas are simple and practical for anyone looking to develop and exceed your customers' expectations. If you want a book that's easy to read and adapt to your business even outside of the travel industry, this will give you ideas to go beyond service."

—Jason Cooper
International Sales Trainer and Coach

You Can't Make This Ship Up is the perfect tell-all for the ultimate cruiser who's looking for the inside scoop on what it's like working on a cruise ship, written by one of the top cruise directors in the industry. The lessons learned can easily be applied, and should be applied to any and all land-based businesses to ensure repeat business and customer loyalty."

—Darryl Dyball
Hospitality Executive

"If you've ever worked at sea or taken a cruise, you won't be able to put it down! An honest, witty and humorous account of the REAL life at sea. It's not all fun and laughter when you're living it, but Paul captures the spirit of cruising with total accuracy. As a VP of a recruitment firm, there are business lessons here for everyone to learn, especially if you have customers!"

—Rachael Fish
Vice President, Bruin Financial

"Paul welcomes you aboard for a voyage to the shores of business excellence. Through a combination of entertaining true stories and keen insights, Paul shares lessons learned from decades of handling the stormiest seas of customer service and delivers you to the sunny shores of success with renewed enthusiasm and a lasting competitive advantage."

—Bruce Gold
Creative Consultant and Entertainer

"A great read for any business executive. I've had the pleasure of sailing with Paul as a guest on board, as well as working with him on land, and his lessons and insights are invaluable to any business. I especially related to the customer experience that businesses must provide, as well as the role of empathy in the corporate world."

—Lisa Scott-Founds
President and CEO, Winterfest, Inc., Home of the Seminole Hard Rock Winterfest Boat Parade

"Paul has done a masterful job of tying entertaining stories about life as a manager on a cruise ship to service and management lessons for any industry. Rather than a dry business book, the result is a most enjoyable read with plenty of lessons built right in."

—Kim Elizabeth Bird
General Manager, African Resorts

"If anyone has a good story to tell, and great lessons to learn, it's Paul. I have had the pleasure of working with Paul numerous times over the past twenty years, from the Caribbean to the Far East, through calm and rough seas—having a great time together!"

—Captain Sindre Borsheim
Royal Caribbean International

You Can't Make This Ship Up:

Business Strategies, Life Lessons and
True Stories From Forty Years at Sea

By Paul Rutter

© Copyright 2021 Paul Rutter

ISBN 978-1-64663-445-3

Published by

köehlerbooks™

3705 Shore Drive
Virginia Beach, VA 23455
800–435–4811
www.koehlerbooks.com

YOU CAN'T MAKE THIS
SHIP UP

PAUL RUTTER

VIRGINIA BEACH
CAPE CHARLES

TABLE OF CONTENTS

FOREWORD

WHEN PAUL RUTTER—*the* Paul Rutter—approached me to write the foreword to his latest book—the book you're reading right now—I was overwhelmed.

Then I noticed the title, *You Can't Make This Ship Up*, and I knew he would be speaking my language. My life, like Paul's, has been defined by the onboard life. Long before I published my first page, I was an onboard entertainer - a magician. It was during those early days that I fell in love with everything about the cruise experience.

I'm a publishing veteran, putting out *Porthole Cruise and Travel* for more than 25 years now. I also produce a YouTube series called *Cruise Control*. But magazines and videos are different creatures entirely than a book like this. A magazine issue lasts for a season, if we're lucky. A YouTube video lasts less than 10 minutes. But a book? A book lasts for a lifetime. Many lifetimes, in fact. I'm flattered to be able to introduce Paul's timeless words of wisdom and his inside scuttlebutt on life at sea.

I knew immediately that no flashy amenity could ever compete with the priceless simplicity of being on a ship, being on the sea, and just being. It's a good life, though it comes with challenges that people working on land might never expect. Hurricanes at your wedding? Brawls in a bingo game? Giving speeches to a naked crowd on a clothing-optional cruise? On a ship, you learn how to deal with all of these, hopefully with style, dignity, compassion, and a great sense of humor. Paul has done all of that! It's the ultimate training for success in any field, including the most important arena of all: Life. I know you will enjoy Paul's unique stories, and the lessons he shares on leadership, the customer experience, and being a decent human being.

Just remember, as my lawyer reminds me, all names have been changed to protect the innocent, and any resemblance between myself and anyone in these pages is purely coincidental.

Happy travels,

Bill Panoff
Editor-in-Chief, *Porthole Cruise and Travel* Magazine

DEDICATION

THIS BOOK IS ESSENTIALLY my love letter to the cruise industry. I have been so blessed to be part of an industry that has taken me to seventy-three (and counting) countries on six continents. And it seems the bucket list keeps growing. But the real heroes of my journey have been the tens of thousands of shipboard crew members from close to a hundred countries I have had the privilege and honor to work with over these past forty-plus years. From Captains to cruise staff, maître d's to musicians, and deckhands to dishwashers, they are some of the hardest working and most dedicated people I have had the good fortune to work alongside. The friends I have made and the relationships that have formed and been nurtured along the way will stay with me forever. The stories I have heard about successes, failures, dreams, and goals have been nothing short of remarkable, and a great source of inspiration.

To the mentors along the way (there have been many), to the people who have taken the time to show me the ropes, and to the teams I have been blessed to lead, thank you, thank you, thank you. This book is dedicated to you.

AUTHOR'S NOTE

I HAVE WORKED for many cruise lines in many positions over my forty-plus year career including Holland America Line®, Costa Cruises®, Royal Caribbean International® and a few other smaller lines. All the stories in this book are true, but the names have been changed to protect the guilty and prevent any unnecessary lawsuits.

INTRODUCTION

THIS BOOK WOULD NOT have been written if I hadn't taken my dog for a walk. She was a beautiful German shepherd, not very big in size, but what she lacked in stature she more than made up for in heart. Her name was Fraulein, and she was the friendliest, most loving dog in the world. (Which is pretty much how everyone describes their dog.)

It was October 1976; I had just graduated Boston University with a degree in education a few months earlier (Go Terriers!), and the weather in Connecticut was starting to turn colder in preparation for the coming winter. I had a part-time job at a large insurance company that was about to end.

We lived across the street from William H. Hall High School, where I graduated four years earlier. This particular afternoon I took Fraulein across the street to the open spaces of the school so she could chase the ball, run around, and get her exercise. She loved doing this, and so did I.

The principal of the high school, Dr. Robert E. Dunn, was walking out the front door on his way to his car and passed by as Fraulein was getting her exercise. We knew each other quite well because I was involved in the award-winning school music program when I was a student. We stopped and chatted for a few minutes, and he asked me what my plans were for the future. Like most twenty-one-year-olds, I didn't have a plan beyond happy hour, but I played it cool.

"I'm planning to do a little traveling across the country before I settle into a job," I mentioned to him. I had already bought a beat-up ten-year-old Volkswagen bus and was planning my trip.

"How would you like to work on a cruise ship?" he asked completely out of the blue.

"Huh, what, are you talking to me?" I asked as I looked around to make sure he was actually addressing his question to me. I had never seen a cruise ship before, and *The Love Boat* was still one year away from network TV. My cruise liner education at this point was anchored in the story of the Titanic, the Queen Mary and the Mayflower. (Okay, not quite a cruise ship as we know it, but you get the idea.)

Dr. Dunn explained there was a parent at the school, Mr. Ziplow, who was starting a new venture, putting some old slot machines on cruise ships, and he needed people to run the operation on board. He had asked Dr. Dunn if he knew any qualified people. Dr. Dunn gave me Mr. Ziplow's phone number, and after calling him, we agreed to meet at the local Friendly's ice cream shop. (If you're from New England, you know Friendly's!) I assume he wanted to test my ability to handle pressure by hosting the interview in the high-stakes landscape of a freezing cold ice cream shop. I shiver now thinking about it.

I met with Earle Ziplow and he explained I would be making change for cruise passengers to play the slot machines. (They would give me a ten dollar bill, and I would give them ten dollars in quarters—not a very difficult, strenuous job.) If I liked the job, he would send me to Las Vegas to learn how to repair the machines if they broke down. These were the old style "one-arm bandit" machines with moving parts where you actually had to pull the handle to get the wheels spinning, much different from the machines today. And did I mention they would send me to LAS VEGAS? They say if you have to bet on anything, bet on yourself. So I rolled the dice and agreed.

Little did I know Dr. Dunn had also recommended a friend of mine, Pat Vaughan, who was already working on board. As luck would have it, Pat and I played Little League baseball together, and

I would be joining him on my first ship, so it was great that I would already know someone on board.

On December 4, 1976, I flew to Ft. Lauderdale, Florida to join the T.S.S. *Fairwind*, a 24,000 gross registered tonnage (GRT) ship sailing for Sitmar Cruises to the Caribbean islands, now long gone. (The ship is long gone, not the Caribbean islands.) It was considered a big ship back in those days, but tiny compared to the 225,000 GRT ships being built now.

Mr. Ziplow asked me to stay on board for at least three months so he could find a replacement, if necessary, to which I agreed. Three months turned into forty years. I have been blessed to be a part of this fascinating industry and watch it grow to tremendous heights, and as they say ... the rest is history!

If I hadn't taken Fraulein for a walk at that particular time on that particular day, my life would be forever changed. I learned valuable lessons from Fraulein that day. Always get your exercise. And always

1977—This tux jacket used to be in style,
I promise.

be on the lookout for new and exciting opportunities that may lead to life-long adventures. You never know when or how they may present themselves to you. Life is way-too-short to stay cooped up inside a house or office all day. Get out and see the world. It's by far the best education you will ever receive.

CHAPTER 1:

ALL ABOARD!

COULD YOU OR YOUR COMPANY survive if you had to live with your customers, clients, and coworkers twenty-four hours a day, seven days a week? Well, that's what life is like for those of us working in the cruise industry. Thousands of officers, staff, and crew spend months at a time on board a cruise ship in close quarters, with a short break on land with our families, then we're back at sea to do it all over again. And our customers are sailing right there with us every day. It's a life we love. I know I do.

As a Cruise Director for the last thirty years, I have learned many lessons about management, leadership, sales and marketing, driving revenue, and, most of all, respect and admiration for the crew members, passengers, and the people who inhabit the places I have visited all over the world. A ship is a microcosm of society and the lessons learned at sea are easily translatable to life and business on land. In fact, I am a frequent speaker and trainer for many companies on how to use the strategies I've developed over the years to improve employee engagement and retention; increase sales; and create not just repeat customers or customers for life, but generational customers.

With it all comes years of amazing stories. I am fortunate enough to spend some of the happiest times of a guest's life with them. For many people, taking a cruise is a dream vacation they have spent a lifetime saving for. We have engagements and weddings on board.

We host family reunions and company retreats. A cruise ship is a happy place.

EXPECT THE UNEXPECTED

As with all service-based businesses, our days come with rewards as well as challenges. The crew is well-trained in exceeding expectations and providing wonderful experiences. One afternoon, Miguel, a newly hired crew member from Portugal, was working the front desk. The day before, a large bridal party had boarded the ship: the bride and groom, the groomsmen, the bridesmaids, and both sides of the family were sailing with us. We were cleared to sail, but had no idea a hurricane had boarded the ship along with the bridal party.

By the next day, we were well underway to the Bahamas. Tamara and Steve, the newlyweds, were making a slow start of it after a big night of celebrating, and around 11:00 a.m. decided to go for a swim on the upper deck. Tamara was ready first in her new bathing suit, hat, and cover-up she had purchased for their honeymoon. Steve, being somewhat hungover, was lagging behind. Ever-patient Tamara, not wanting to push Steve (after all, it *was* their first day as husband and wife) but eager to catch some rays, told Steve, "No problem, honey. If you don't mind, though, I think I'll head up first and grab a couple of lounge chairs for us. Just come find me as soon as you get changed."

Steve readily agreed.

Tamara picked up her hat and her straw bag, left the room, and took the elevator to the deck two flights above. It was a picture-perfect day for the start of their honeymoon. The sun was shining, the ocean was calm, and Tamara found two chaise lounges right next to the pool, not too far from the bar. She got out her towel and draped it across the second chaise to save it for Steve. Then she sat down and began to search through her bag. She pulled out her sunglasses and the paperback book she had brought along. She would wait until Steve joined her before ordering a cocktail.

After about fifteen minutes, Tamara noticed two things: She had forgotten to pack her sunscreen into her bag, and Steve still had not shown up. No problem. She would just call Steve from the phone at the bar, find out what was holding him up (had he fallen asleep after she left?), and ask him to please bring the sunscreen with him.

Steve didn't pick up. *Maybe he's on the way*, Tamara thought.

Another 10 minutes passed and no Steve.

With a sigh, not knowing whether to be concerned or miffed, Tamara stood up, grabbed her bag, and marched back to the elevator, down two flights, and back to the room to see what was going on.

Poor Miguel had no idea any of this had transpired twenty minutes later when Tamara came huffing, full steam toward the front desk. Flanked on either side of Tamara were her brothers and parents.

Barefoot, hair askew, and with a red, tear-soaked face, Tamara stopped two feet in front of the desk, pulled off her wedding ring, hurled it toward the unsuspecting Miguel, and yelled, "Get me off this f'ing ship! Now!"

As Miguel was soon to find out, although it was somewhat difficult to get Tamara to calm down enough to speak coherently, Tamara had found her new husband, still in the room. He had not changed into his swim trunks. In fact, he had not changed into anything; he was quite naked when Tamara found him—on top of the maid of honor.

Tamara and her family debarked the ship at the next port of call. The groom and his family remained on board for the rest of the cruise. I'm not too sure about the maid of honor.

That's one way to rock the boat.

∞ ∞ ∞

GETTING TO KNOW YOU

When you are hundreds of miles from shore and people's lives are in your hands, decisions must be made swiftly. It truly is sink or swim out there. What I'll be sharing with you in the pages that follow are processes that the cruise industry has developed over the years that deal with everything from hiring to firing, difficult guests, weather and health emergencies, and never-ending ways to entertain the passengers. Your business may be able to benefit from the policies and processes that the cruise industry has put into place.

These processes have developed from the welcome input of everyone involved. Passenger questionnaires, crew experience, and management listening skills, are all part of the way we lead, sell, serve, and grow.

In my first book, *Repeat Business Inc: The Business of Staying in Business*, I talk about More Than Perfect® customer service. Spending twenty-four hours a day on board with our passengers led me to develop a proactive state of mind. Consistently reaching for greater achievements in customer service is the foundation of creating a More Than Perfect® experience. This experience gives your team and company a competitive advantage and customer base that will continue a relationship with you for years to come.

In my business, my coworkers are called "crew." You may refer to the people you spend most of your day with as staff, employees, or team members. Whatever term you use, and whatever industry you are in, these people are the backbone of any business. Now, in *You Can't Make This Ship Up*, I am going behind the scenes to explore ways we can create a More Than Perfect® experience for them, too.

More Than Perfect®
Memorable – Make it memorable.
Original – Offer something original.
Repeat – Repeat your successes.
Exceed – Exceed everyone's expectations.
*Always deliver **MORE**.*

To quote Sir Richard Branson of Virgin Group, "Clients do not come first. Employees come first. If you take care of your employees, they will take care of the clients."

For that reason, we will begin with addressing a business's most valued asset, it's employees. The first few chapters address issues with finding, onboarding, and retaining the most qualified and valuable people.

Some issues, such as safety and security, are of equal concern to employees and customers alike, and therefore I address those next in the book.

Finally, there is a lot to share about treating the customers right and keeping them coming back.

If you are a life-long cruiser or have ever wondered if what you saw on *The Love Boat* could have been true, you will be entertained by these stories I've collected over the years. Do people really fall overboard? What happens during a hurricane or major storm? Do you do burials at sea? Is there really only one bartender on board?

For those of you in human resources and leadership roles, you will learn effective and often creative ways to keep your teams healthy and happy. The sales and client management folks will learn some really out-of-the-box ideas for attracting and retaining clients. And for those of you just entering the workforce, may what you learn here make for smooth sailing in your career.

So, get comfortable and read on. If you think you recognize someone in the story, rest assured, I have changed all the names, with the exception of those I quote directly with their permission.

I'll be sharing even more interesting stories, because . . . you really *can't* make this ship up!

SHIP TO SHORE

In the chapters that follow, we will explore how lessons learned at sea can easily be applied in a land-based or virtual business. These lessons will be the lifejackets you need when you feel like your business is drowning. Unlike Jack and Rose, there will actually be enough life jackets for everyone.

CHAPTER 2:

FRESH OFF THE BOAT:
HOW TO HIRE EFFECTIVELY

NOT EVERYBODY ATTENDS a job interview in an ice cream shop. The interview process is much more complicated, regimented, streamlined, mandated, and virtual these days. Yet one thing remains the same. According to a LinkedIn survey, roughly eighty-five percent of jobs are filled through networking. Yes, it still boils down to "who you know," but that's just an applicant's first step, the step that gets them in the door. There are still many hurdles to cross before making a hire.

Applicants undergo a battery of different tests: cognitive, personality type, integrity, skills assessment, physical ability. And nearly fifty percent of all employers employ some type of personality or psychological test as part of the job application process. There are tests that can measure extraversion, stress tolerance, and even agreeableness.

Even with all of these scientifically-designed, computerized tests, there comes a time for human interaction. Now granted, that is not always in-person and across a desk anymore. It is more likely to be on a video teleconference. Still, at some point, a human has to make a decision on whom to hire.

Your applicant has passed a cognitive test, their personality test shows them to be outgoing, and their resume includes all the right words to match the job description. It's relatively easy to look good on paper, especially with the proliferation of professional resume writing services out there. A job application can include the right schools, the right experience, and the proper number of recommendations. But what about the things that aren't reflected in a resume or cover letter? Enthusiasm? Compassion? Willingness to learn? As a leader, you can recognize the existence of these qualities and encourage them.

HAVE A CONVERSATION

When making your hiring decision, look beyond the resumes and tests. Engage your applicant in conversation. Skip the canned hiring questions everyone has prepared for. Instead of asking why they left their last job, ask how they got it. Ask them about what they do on their weekends. Go off script. When your applicant feels comfortable, she is likely to share more about what she likes to do, what makes her happy. Those non-job specific attitudes and activities offer clues for where and how this person may fit into your organization. Do they coach a kids' soccer team? Then they are likely to have patience and understand the importance of rules and possess the potential for leadership. Does your applicant sing in the church choir? Then she/he is likely to understand the importance of working as a team for a perfect outcome.

As someone who is in the position to hire, you will meet people who are just entering the workforce. You may see talent and potential in them that they do not realize yet. Your job as a leader is to build other leaders.

You can teach a skill, but you cannot teach someone to have a good attitude. Either they do or they don't. Hiring for attitude over a skill set is very important to talk about in business. It's critical to stress to leaders and to remind people who want to be in leadership positions that attitude is vital to advancement.

I have worked for several global cruise lines with thousands of employees, both shipboard and shore-side. With numbers that large, applicants are pre-screened by job placement agencies that sift through hundreds of online applications before choosing a person to send on board. I do not do any of the hiring for my division: it is done by a shore-side Human Resources (HR) team. The folks they hire become my responsibility as soon as they walk up the gangway.

Q&A SAVES THE DAY

There are so many things an HR agent is not allowed to ask because of hiring fairness policies. And I agree with most of them. "Are you married?" "How old are you?" "Coke or Pepsi?" (Okay I made that up.) However, there needs to be some kind of engagement to figure out how that person is going to fit into your environment. They can be perfectly wonderful people, but not be a good fit.

When you are in the position of hiring, think of questions that relate to the position that will encourage people to relate scenarios from past experiences. Do your best to keep the tone conversational so that you don't sound like you are reading generic questions out of a management manual. "What is your weakest skill that you would like to improve?" That's been overused. Every applicant has looked it up on the internet to see the right way to answer. Their answers are going to be as canned and insincere as that question.

Instead, relate a common challenge the candidate is likely to face in the position for which you are hiring. For instance, an HR Manager for an insurance company may ask, "Sometimes our underwriters are very slow to get us the information we need to put together a quote for our clients. They leave us with very little time to reply by the deadline. Have you had something similar happen in your previous job?"

The answer will reveal a number of things, including compassion and understanding. "Yes, it happens sometimes, and it really does put me under a time crunch. But I know the underwriter is absolutely swamped and she is working as fast as she can. I deal with it by having as much information ready ahead of time, so all I have to do is plug in her numbers when they get to me." Your applicant's response reveals that they plan ahead for contingency.

Someone else may respond with, "Yes, Bill does it to me all the time. I swear he singles me out just for the pleasure of watching me panic. I have to work late to finish up my contracts." Although this person shows you that they are willing to put in extra time to get their job done, you may want to consider that this person sees himself as a victim. The victim mentality tends to look for someone else to blame which can build resentments toward coworkers, whether warranted or not.

There used to be a position on board a while ago called the social hostess. She was considered the "first lady" of the ship. She would introduce the Captain at the Captain's Cocktail Reception. She facilitated weddings, planned group functions, greeted guests, answered questions—a very front-of-house sophisticated position.

One afternoon, our social hostess, Barbara, struck up a conversation with me as we passed each other in the hallway. I'd known Barbara casually for the three years she had been with the company and she always struck me as being efficient and professional. In the course of our conversation about the smooth seas and the new menu items, she said, "God, I can't stand talking to these passengers."

My jaw must have dropped open and I responded, "You are the social hostess. What do you mean you can't stand talking to the passengers? That's the main part of your job—talking to the passengers."

Completely unaware of the shock that must have been evident in my tone, she responded: "They act like such privileged tourists. They ask the same questions over and over. Do you know how sick I get of explaining to them not everyone gets to have dinner with the Captain?"

I made my excuses and got away from Barbara and the awkward conversation as quickly as possible. I do admit to watching her interactions with guests more closely over the rest of that cruise season. She continued to behave as a professional, but I always wondered what seething resentment lay beneath that forced smile. By the next year, Barbara had left the company, hopefully to move on to a position better suited to her strengths.

The same approach for seeking out the right attitude in new hires needs to be carried over to promoting as well. Years of service should not be given more weight than aptitude for the job.

In the mid-nineties, cruise lines began expanding very rapidly. For example, Royal Caribbean launched six new ships in three years. Every six months they would come out with a new ship, which means every six months they had to hire and train close to 900 new crew members. They would take some experienced crew members from every ship in the fleet, along with a few new hires onto a brand new ship. You don't want a new ship with all new hires. Likewise, you don't want to expand too rapidly if you don't have the proper personnel in order to facilitate that strategy.

Many people get a job on board and want to switch departments. Most cruise lines require a crew member to complete a full contract before they are considered for a different position. They may be hired as a cleaner, but that cleaner then sees what the cruise staff does and says, "Oh, I'm a dancer and host karaoke back home, I'd like to join the cruise staff team." There is a process to go through, and then they are interviewed to see if it's a good fit.

Just like an initial hire, it is important to make sure that someone's personality, work ethic, and values fit your company's culture.

Hiring the first person that comes along because you haven't done your homework, can get you in trouble. Likewise, when you're hiring just anybody because of time constraints, that can be worse in the long run, because it costs your company so much more to replace them.

It's a minimum of twenty-five percent just to replace the organizational intelligence that walks out the door, then another ten to fifteen percent to woo and train a new hire. For example, according to the Society for Human Resource Management (SHRM), a $60,000 salary can cost up to forty percent to replace, which is about $24,000. That $60,000 salary just cost the company $84,000. They may recover it once the employee has been there for three to five years. Leadership often forgets these costs when thinking about how to move an organization forward.

This is the problem of only looking at the analytics. Yes, the applicant has checked all the boxes, but you need to have that face-to-face experience to understand if someone is a good fit. Sometimes you shouldn't make hiring decisions based on pure logic. If you hire the wrong person in March and you have to rehire in May, that money is completely lost. Plus, the workload has to be distributed among the people who are already doing their jobs. That in turn can cause resentments and overworking of the remaining staff.

TAKE A WALK

As part of the application process, some land-based businesses will actually take applicants for a tour around the facility, giving them the opportunity to meet and talk with the employees. The person doing the hiring will later talk to those employees and ask, "Okay, what'd you think of this person? We're thinking of hiring them." Seriously consider the responses of people who will be working directly with the new hire. Those folks will have a much better understanding of what the position requires than someone from a different department. Consider the team dynamic. It's not just having one more confident person in a group of extroverts. Introverts and extroverts complement each other very well. Every business needs different personalities on their team in order to make it run smoothly and efficiently. Look deeper into the motivations and work ethic your group shares.

Having a new hire fit in with the team is a critical dynamic that can't be overlooked.

Helping someone else grow in their career can benefit you as well. This is another opportunity that would serve you well to recognize. If you have your eyes on a different position, you are more likely to be considered for that promotion or transfer if you can show management that you have someone ready to assume your current role—someone you have trained.

ENTITLEMENT WILL SINK YOUR SHIP

One time, there were two staff members who wanted to be promoted to Assistant Cruise Director (ACD). Victor *expected* to be promoted. He had been with the company for five years, felt that he was the best thing since sliced bread, and fully believed that he should be promoted above everybody else, just because he had been there the longest. He did his job, but wasn't really interested in helping the team as a whole. He complained about other staff members he felt didn't live up to his standards, but never went out of his way to help them improve.

James also wanted to be an Assistant Cruise Director. He had only been on the ship for two years yet had a completely different attitude. He came to me and said, "I'm really interested in moving up and will do whatever is necessary to be considered. I want to learn as much as I possibly can to get the position, so I've been coming in an hour early to get more exposure to what the ACD does. I'm also staying on duty later and offering to help with any tasks that can use another pair of hands."

James is the one I pushed for promotion. Victor, although very efficient in his current position, expected the promotion as a logical next step, but his attitude and approach of "it better go to me" was not what we were looking for. Whereas James had the attitude of, "Whatever you need from me, I'm here to help and improve the team." They both were very good, but James was promoted because he had a much more open and positive attitude, as well as the better team approach.

SHIP TO SHORE

The lessons from these stories can easily be applied in a land-based or virtual business. Here's how to find and hire the More Than Perfect® applicant:

- During the interview, ask the potential hire to share a favorite memory of their last job, or an experience that is related to the position you are filling.
- If they bring Twinkies, ask the potential hire to share those as well.
- Give the interviewee an example of how to make the position their own. Is there room for any creativity—from the freedom to decorate an office, to helping choose a yearly fundraiser?
- Repeat your successes. If you find your best hires have a particular major in college, or have experience as camp counselors, look for that quality in future hires.

Having the patience to make the right hire for the right position saves time and money and makes the experience better for every member of the team. No one wants to work beside someone they want to throw overboard.

CHAPTER 3:

SHAPE UP OR SHIP OUT: SETTING EXPECTATIONS FOR YOUR TEAM

DEPENDING ON THE SHIP, there can be between seventy-five and 200 crew members within the Cruise Division (the division I manage) and they may come from fifteen to twenty different countries. On board the entire ship, depending on the size, there are anywhere from 800 to 2,200 crew members representing over seventy different countries. What a wonderful experience to be a part of this diverse, cultural smorgasbord.

As a Cruise Director and division head, I like to personally greet all new hires in my division on their first day on board. I call them into my office, and we have a chat. I officially welcome them to the team, and we spend about five minutes together.

All new hires have been told well ahead of time what clothes to bring, what uniforms are required, and what they will need for certain theme nights. They have received the company literature about the activities on board and what they can expect to learn. But stepping onto the ship and sailing away from the port makes it all real and is quite literally a dramatic departure.

Despite the preparation, new hires are still pretty nervous, so in order to get them to relax a little, I start by asking them, "Where are you from?" Then, I follow that up with, "Are you ready to go home yet?" That usually gets a little nervous laugh out of them and I go on to explain that everybody's first day is crazy. Undeniably hectic. You walk on a ship and you're in a crew area, seeing everybody flying by, carrying big crates of food and luggage and supplies, and you're thinking to yourself, *Holy crap, what did I get myself into here?* And everybody thinks like that. I tell them, "Take a deep breath. Have you gotten to the point where you're thinking to yourself, this is the biggest mistake of my life?" And pretty much everybody answers, "Yeah. Yeah. That's exactly what I was thinking."

I reassure them that we've all felt that way. Being away from home, being away from family, and learning all the ins and outs of a new job can be daunting and can make people feel as if they are completely on their own. It is important to assure them that they will have support, and I say, "We're here to make sure that you're successful. If you're not successful, we're not doing our job very well."

As the division head, it's my responsibility to give everyone on my team the tools they need to do their job. I emphasize, "There will be lots of training on board to make sure you're successful. Once you get through the first month, you'll be fine. If you have any problems, you now know where my office is, and my door is always open."

A few years ago, a guy named Peter, who got my five-minute welcome speech about five years before, was back on board. He walked into my office on his very first day with the company as a Video Technician, and today he is a Broadcast Manager, in charge of the entire shipboard broadcast operation. He came up to me and said, "You know, you did something that I've never forgotten."

And I asked, "Oh really, what was that?"

"You took time out of your busy day, my first day on board. You asked me to come to your office and you officially welcomed me on board. And I'm thinking, the Cruise Director, the head of the division, has welcomed me into his office. I was so impressed."

I wasn't doing it to impress people. I was doing it because I knew it would help them adjust.

He went on to say, "I was so impressed that I now do that in my role. Anytime somebody is brand new, I bring them into my office to officially welcome them."

Prior to this conversation, I had never thought my five-minute talk was a big deal. It was just my way of making the newcomers feel welcome. Peter's comments drove home for me that you never know when somebody is watching what you do. You can have a positive or a negative influence on somebody, and odds are you're never going to know about it. For that reason, be mindful of the way you may come across to others. Choose to always be professional and responsible. It will serve you well.

According to Zenefits, an HR and payroll benefits company, "employees who participate in a structured onboarding program are sixty-nine percent more likely to stay with an organization for three years." The old nautical phrase, "Shape up or ship out" has been long used as an ultimatum, but how can someone "shape up" if they don't know what is expected of them? Clearly broadcasting the rules and expectations falls squarely on the shoulders of leadership and management. If your employees don't know what your requirements are, they cannot be expected to meet them.

During my welcome conversation, I inform our new hires that they will be assigned a buddy. They will shadow this more experienced team member for the first two weeks aboard. All they need to do is just watch, listen, ask questions, take notes, and absorb. The cruise staff will learn how to host many activities, including trivia, bingo, and dance classes, as well as where all the equipment is stored and how to use it. Most cruise lines offer theme night parties, and the cruise staff perform various dances; either it's a line dance, or the latest club dance, which they will also learn.

IS IT A GOOD FIT?

Every new hire is on a ninety-day probationary period, which is something I recommend to all companies regardless of size. This policy benefits both employer and employee to make sure the person, the company, and the position are all a good fit. It's a good idea to hand a blank evaluation to any new person who joins your team so they will see exactly what they will be evaluated on during the ninety-day period. We also supply a copy of the review we give our team members at the end of their contract.

Cruise lines have a disciplinary system in place as well. On the first minor offense, the crew member and supervisor sit down and talk. This gives the employee notice that they have strayed from the rules and procedures and gives them an opportunity to explain their actions.

The conversation is noted, dated, and both the employee and manager sign. Infractions may include things like being late to report for work, rudeness to a guest, or being out of uniform.

All crew members are required to be set up and ready to start fifteen minutes early for events and performances. More often than not, there are no problems and everyone accomplishes set-up very quickly. This leaves plenty of time for the cruise staff member to meet, socialize, and answer questions from the guests.

Whether you are running a business at sea or on land, the same principles apply to employee onboarding. The first two to four weeks that an employee is with your company sets the tone. You want that person to be successful. To assure this, do a thirty-, sixty- and ninety-day evaluation so they can see how they're doing and have the opportunity to alter their course if need be. At the end of the ninety-day probation, if they're not happy with their job, they can leave. If you're not happy with them, you can send them home for any reason—no harm, no foul. But there needs to be documentation.

No matter the size of your company, instituting a ninety-day probationary period with regular evaluations will greatly enhance the organization's culture. It ensures the company and the new hire are a good fit and it provides an opportunity for new people to adjust to your culture. On board a ship, it isn't just the corporate culture the crew needs to adjust to, there are the languages, lifestyles, and attitudes of people from close to seventy different countries—

for some it is the first time they have encountered such a diverse population.

Communication is key. With rules and guidelines regularly updating, it's important to keep everyone informed. I prefer to meet with my senior managers every cruise, and the entire division once a month. We cover everything from crew boat drills to crew parties. (Or as we like to call them, team-building get-togethers.)

During these divisional meetings, I try to emphasize the positive, welcoming aspect of what we do. I always tell the team, "We're not just cruise staff, youth staff, or sports staff. We're public relations experts and we create memories. We are impacting people's lives in a way that we may never know about, so it's important for us to be warm and friendly to everyone. Make sure to try and acknowledge each person with a sincere greeting, even if it's just a quick, 'Hello.' It's important our guests feel welcome during all aspects of their stay with us."

Being nice to people can be a big ask. In the cruise industry, we do the same thing week after week. For instance, let's say it's a seven-day cruise with the same itinerary, week after week, for months at a time, we do the exact same thing. But, it is always day one for our guests.

This means we get asked the same questions over and over, as well as some strange requests. Sometimes you want to throw up your hands and say, "How can people be so clueless? No, you cannot water ski off the back of the ship, no matter how good you are. That would not lead to a happy ending." Although it might help thin the herd a little. I remind my people that even if you hear the craziest question, you need to respond as if it is a perfectly rational request that you are happy to answer.

I have a whole list of silly questions we've been asked over the years—and asked more than once. Such as:

- "Will Alaska accept US dollars?" I believe so, the last time I checked they were part of the US.

- "Does the crew live on board?" No, we commute.
- "Is that salt water or fresh water in the toilets?" Not sure to be honest, I've never tasted it.
- "Why are the ruins (in Rome) in such poor condition?" Umm, maybe because they're ruins.
- "Is this island completely surrounded by water?" That would be a yes, that's why it's called an island.
- "What do you do with the ice carvings, once they melt?" Take showers with them, of course.
- Asked to the photo manager: "How do we know which photographs are ours?" Really? Look for your face.
- One guest asked why her inside cabin had no windows for her to look at the ocean. Maybe because it's an "inside" cabin?
- "Will I get wet if I go on the snorkel tour?" Only if you go snorkeling.
- One guest went on a beach tour in the Caribbean, but complained she didn't enjoy it "because there was too much sand on the beach." Well, that's a good place for it.
- A cute question from a six-year old, "Has this ship ever sunk before?" Let's hope not.
- And of course, the granddaddy of them all, "What time is the midnight buffet?"

SOLID GOLD STANDARDS: WHY THIS IS IMPORTANT

To help set excellent standards and expectations for employees to follow, many businesses come up with corporate policies in the form of an acronym. For example, Royal Caribbean International developed a policy called Gold Anchor Standards for customer service. This policy guide had four key pillars. **G O L D**.

G is Greet and Smile. It is part of your job, anytime you are within ten feet of another person, crew or guest, you must acknowledge them. You don't have to stop and have a conversation. You don't have to find out their whole life history. You just don't ignore them as if they don't exist. You just give a nod, a smile, and say, "Hello. Good morning. Nice to see you," and keep going on your way. This practice has been introduced to land-based hospitals with great success. It is a proven morale booster, even in that serious, stressful environment.

O is Own the Experience. If somebody comes to you with a problem, you don't say, "Oh, that's not my job. That's somebody else's job." Once that person comes to you, you own it. You have to do whatever it takes to get that problem solved. Now, if that means you take a customer personally to the front desk to say, "These are the people who will be able to help you," then that's owning the experience. Obviously, everybody can't do everything. A cabin steward can't cook a meal for you, but they definitely know who can or who to ask. You may not be able to arrange a refund for someone, but you can find out who can arrange it. That is your way of owning it.

The **L** is for Look the Part. Everyone working on a cruise ship is required to wear a uniform of one sort or another. There are even day uniforms and night uniforms, whether it is the Captain with his or her hat and epaulets or the galley staff with their white toques and different colored bandanas. We may have stricter rules and dress codes than other businesses, but every company has standards or should create them to set expectations for their employees. Our crew members have to be properly dressed, in the correct uniform, with name tag in place and the daily program in their possession. This ensures they are instantly identifiable to the guests and able to answer any questions about the day's activities.

There are grooming standards, as well. How many piercings you can wear in each ear, exposure of tattoos, how short your skirt can be, even the length of goatees is described in the dress code. In the service industry, uniforms help guests recognize staff to seek their assistance, thereby making the customer experience smoother.

D is Deliver the WOW. Delivering the wow doesn't have to take vast amounts of time, expense, or energy. Sometimes it's just a matter of thoughtfulness, and it will leave a lasting, positive impression on your customer. Can you remember someone's drink order? Do you inquire about the turnout of their child's soccer game? Even saying, "Happy Birthday" can create a positive experience for your customer. What are some low or no-cost steps you can take to deliver the WOW in your business?

The **G O L D** policies and practices are easily applicable to your business as well. Feel free to adopt them or use them as inspiration for developing your own. Creating a standard of practice accomplishes two things: a better experience for your customer and a clear set of expectations for your staff. It also eliminates uncomfortable conversations when policies are clearly laid out in advance. It eliminates the possibility of managers exercising their personal opinions on a case-by-case basis.

Many cruise lines also have what I call "The Big Book of How to Run a Cruise Line." It details everything an employee needs to know. It's impossible to know everything in the book, as there is so much information, but with the "search" function, one can easily find anything they are looking for. It is a living, breathing document that is constantly being updated, and is usually kept on everyone's computer for easy access. At Princess Cruises, it is called the *Hotel Rules and Regulations* manual. At Royal Caribbean, it is the *Safety and Quality Management* manual, or *SQM*, and is used to make sure the product stays consistent throughout the fleet. Our "Boat Bible" if you will.

The *SQM* manual has come to the rescue on many occasions. It clarifies policies and procedures and stops any misunderstandings in their tracks. The rules, procedures, and company forms found within its pages keep everyone rowing in the same direction.

Katelyn, a young lady from the sports staff, came into my office one day to say she thought she was being treated unfairly. She didn't think it should be part of her job to perform what we call "doing the doors."

"Doing the doors" means greeting people as they come into the theater at night for the show. "Hello, welcome. Hope you had a nice day." Just greeting guests with a smile. It's a socializing thing and lasts about 30 minutes. The cruise division are the people out front, the socializers, the fun people who lead the activities, so it's part of our job. Well, Katelyn didn't think it was part of *her* job. She said she was hired as sports staff so why should she have to stand at the doors? It should be a cruise staff responsibility. And so I said, "Okay, are you familiar with your job description? Have you ever seen your job description?" And she replied, "I can't even remember."

I can assure you, yes, she did know her job description. Every manager is required to review the job description on the first day a new hire steps on board. It's company policy.

Inside, I'm thinking, *Really? You don't want to have to say hello to people? Today we're in Japan and next month we're in Australia or the Caribbean or Alaska. How many of your friends would change places with you in a heartbeat? And you're complaining that you have to stand at a door and greet people?*

But what I *said* was, "Well, let's look at the *SQM* manual, and check your job description. If it's not in there, then of course, we're not going to make you do anything that the company says you don't have to do." *Like smiling.*

I already knew the answer of course, but by bringing up the *SQM* manual, it showed that I was giving the question consideration and that I alone was not making an arbitrary decision. "Let's go through it all," I said, and read the description aloud, which mapped out everything that's expected of her, right there in black and white. Sure enough, her duties included socializing with the guests at night.

And that solved that.

Surprisingly, only about twenty-five percent of companies have an up-to-date employee or corporate handbook, which can protect against legal action for wrongful termination or discrimination. In it you can share your mission and vision statements, as well as a reminder of the expectations and tone of your company. Can you imagine how many fewer trips there would be to the HR office if every employee had a handbook to reference?

Having policies in place builds the foundation of your company culture and culture is extremely important. According to a Gallup poll, seventy to eighty percent of the workforce does not look forward to going to work, which is a real shame. We should all look forward to going to work. We have to wake up in the morning and welcome what the day brings. That's the key. And that's where the training comes in. You have to create a culture where everyone looks forward to getting to work and contributing. Make people feel appreciated. Recognize not only what they have brought to the job but also what they have learned while they are there. People want to know that their work has meaning and has value.

The "Boat Bible" manuals contain more than job descriptions. It is the source for assuring that the product stays consistent throughout the fleet. It's like McDonald's. You can go into a McDonald's anywhere in the world and have the exact same experience. Okay, maybe that's not the best example for a cruise line. Let's change that to if you stay in any Ritz-Carlton hotel in the world, you can expect the same standard of excellence. And that's the same standard we wanted for our cruise line. The details and specifications in the *SQM* manual assure that no matter what ship you sail on with them, you're going to get the same excellent Royal Caribbean experience that they promote and are known for.

YOU EAT HOW MUCH?

These manuals also cover product consistency, which is so important to the customer experience. For example, all of the food is procured from the same sources and shipped all over the world. The ships do not buy their own food at different ports around the world, because you don't know the quality you're going to get. They do make an exception for fresh produce, if needed. They know exactly how much beef, chicken, and fish is needed for a seven or fourteen-day cruise because they have all the statistics from previous cruises. They have computer programs that track use and consumption, which helps reduce waste. They project seasonal differences as well. They know that during the summer, more kids will be sailing, so they make sure to get more hot dogs and hamburgers and french fries. Because again, they want to exceed expectations. And the only way they can do that is for everyone to be on the same page, delivering the same product, working towards the same goals. Passengers can expect the same wonderful experience from ship to ship and so can the crew.

Here is a brief, unofficial summary of how much food is eaten on a typical seven-day cruise, depending on the cruise line and ship size:

15,000 to 20,000 pounds of beef
10,000 to 12,000 pounds of chicken
40,000 to 50,000 eggs
20,000 pounds of potatoes
12,000 pounds of fish
2,000 pounds of lobster
700 pounds of ice cream
6,000 to 7,000 bottles of wine
30,000 to 40,000 bottles of beer
Two pounds of fruits and veggies (okay, that's a lie, it's more like 60,000 pounds.)

CELEBRATE YOUR DIFFERENCES

I've shared processes by which we familiarize our new hires with their new life on board. Equally important is preparing our current crew for the newcomers. Existing crew know what it's like to be the new person, trying to learn so many things very quickly. With prior knowledge, everyone can plan accordingly.

Ships are the perfect venue for experiencing cultural diversity. Passengers and crews alike have the opportunity to meet people from all over the world. Some may not have travelled outside of their own country before, and they will gain exposure to many different cultures during their stay on board. The crew will work and live with people who have completely different religious and political beliefs. This can be a positive, life-changing experience for those who embrace it.

SHIP TO SHORE

The lessons from these stories can easily be applied in a land-based or virtual business. Here's how:

- If you haven't begun to intentionally create a company culture, I suggest the Acronym Exercise, which is the kind of exercise that doesn't require a yoga mat, a Peleton, or any sweating whatsoever. I mentioned earlier about Gold Anchor Standards, **G O L D**. Start by thinking of some of the key values you want to express. What are some of the ways you can serve your customers? As you work through the answers to those questions, you'll be surprised how quickly you come up with your own acronym.
- Choose a word that is seven letters or less so that it is easy to remember. Get everybody involved with the project. Remember, being part of the process helps everyone buy into shared goals they helped create. Then post your acronym and its meaning for your staff and your customers to see.
- Your acronym should represent your core values and make them easier to remember. If people don't remember or aren't reminded of them, they won't follow them every day.

CHAPTER 4:
WHEN YOUR SHIP COMES IN: JUMP ABOARD

YOU ARE ALLOWED TO THINK bigger than where you are.

Sometimes in life, things don't always work out as planned. (How's that for an understatement?) And sometimes in life, things work out better than planned. Whether you're a manager, a new hire, or someone looking to join an industry, don't limit yourself to any preconceived notions about your potential. In the cruise industry, the time between applying for a job and being placed in one can range anywhere from one week to over a year. There are visas to apply for and physicals to pass. Sometimes positions are filled right away because it just happens that the timing was right, that somebody on board was let go and needs to be replaced right away, or someone has transferred to another ship or position. If an applicant happens to have the right visas and can pass a physical examination, they can be placed rather quickly in a position for which they may *not* have applied.

In order to attract the best talent, many cruise lines use hiring partners in more than forty countries around the world including India, China, the Philippines, Indonesia, Portugal, South Africa, Italy, Israel, and of course the United States and Canada, amongst others. Hiring partners are third party companies that recruit and pre-screen applicants. Partners earn their commission per individual placed only after that hire has successfully completed ninety days on board. If somebody is fired within the first ninety days, the hiring partners don't make their commission. Therefore, they want to place the right applicant in the right position.

In order to fill a vacancy quickly and get on track for payment, someone could be assigned as an assistant waiter who has never worked in a restaurant before. If a person is willing to learn, they can overcome inexperience. Remember, many people will take any job just to get on board and get their foot in the door so they can work their way into the position they really want. As the saying goes, "Hire for attitude, train for skill."

There are always far more applicants (qualified and otherwise) to apply than there are positions available, and the hiring partner may channel an applicant to a different position. For instance, someone may apply for a stateroom attendant position. If there are better qualified applicants for that position, the hiring partner will offer the person the opportunity to interview for a cleaner position instead. "We have no open positions like the one you applied for, but we do have a different housekeeping position open. You can be a cleaner on board." In any industry, don't fall into the trap of thinking a lesser assignment is your only potential. You are allowed to think bigger than where you are.

Many people consider working on a cruise ship a very exciting career option and they dream of becoming an Executive Chef, Food and Beverage Director, Executive Housekeeper or a Marine Officer. They are willing to take any job offered, just to get hired and get on board. Crew members who aren't happy with the first job they get still must do an exceptional job if they want a great evaluation, which in turn will help them move into the position they are really aiming for.

START SMALL AND GROW BIG

Some of the best workers I've had in the Cruise Division have come from other divisions on board. It could be a dishwasher who is good at fixing things, and we put them backstage and they're one of the best backstage hands we have, because they're really passionate about following that path, as opposed to the one they were originally given as a cleaner or a dishwasher.

Charles is a great example of someone who worked his way up. He originally started in the galley, became a member of the stage staff production team, and is now a Production Manager, in charge of the entire backstage area and running the shows. He proved himself every step of the way.

I recently worked with a lady from China on my last ship. Li Wei came on as a cleaner, but happened to be a wonderful dancer and singer, as well. She finished her first contract and then came back and applied to come over to cruise staff. In less than eighteen months, she had worked her way up from a starting position as a cleaner to the career she trained for and dreamed of. She is absolutely one of the best cruise staff members I've worked with.

If you don't get what you wanted first, but really have a desire to work in a certain position, then you sometimes have to go through some trials. Consider taking the initial offer in order to make yourself known and begin establishing your reputation as an excellent worker.

Even if you're not in the position you ultimately want to end up with, you still need to do a great job because you don't know who's watching, and you never know what a good evaluation, recommendation, or referral can lead to.

Here's another story for you. We used to have a passenger talent show every cruise. People would do magic tricks, or play an instrument, maybe dance, and at every performance, a few people would sing. It was all in good fun, and no one took themselves too seriously. The crew and audience would applaud politely after each performance and up would come the next guest.

One night, a young woman named Helen walked onto the stage, sat down at the piano, played a few slow bars and began to sing "Killing Me Softly," by Roberta Flack. By the time she got to the words,

"Singing my life with his words," the audience was mesmerized. Helen's voice rang clear and smooth above the gentle cacophony of clinking glasses, and she received the biggest round of applause when the song ended. A few of the passengers asked me afterward if she was one of our professional performers. The next day I found her during lunch and said, "Listen Helen, you are a phenomenal singer. Have you ever thought about working on a cruise ship? We'd love to have you on our team." And about six months later, after she went through the hiring process, she did wind up joining our company in the entertainment department.

Now this doesn't happen often, but it has happened, and I know a few people who have been hired this way. We'll go to them and say, "Listen, you're a wonderful singer." Or, "You're a talented dancer." We invite them to submit an audition tape to become one of the cast members. So, it does happen; guests on board have been offered jobs. We even had a Cruise Director who was "discovered" at the talent show!

The point of this story is whatever you do, do it well, even if it is an amateur talent show. You never know what opportunities may open up to you. There's a famous adage: "The way you do one thing is how you do everything." Establish your reputation as somebody who's reliable, responsible, and professional. Do the job you have today to the best of your ability, and remember, even the things you do for fun can open up tremendous possibilities.

NOT THE WAY WE PLANNED IT

We don't all start out at the top with magnificent success. Carnival Cruise Lines was founded by Ted Arison in 1972. The *Mardi Gras* was his very first ship and on its maiden voyage out of the port of Miami, it ran aground on a sandbar. Things didn't really start out as he wanted, but over the years, Arison and Carnival launched thirty-three ships. Arison took the company public in 1987 and went on to become one of the richest men in the world.

When Arison brought his son, Micky, into the business, he made him do many different jobs on board. Employees are particularly skeptical of nepotism. "Oh, you're only here because you're the owner's son. You don't know what this is like."

Micky went on board as a dishwasher. He knew how to be a cog. By learning and knowing all the various jobs within the company, he was able to lead as a CEO a lot better than somebody who just came in, started at the top, and didn't really know the whole business from the ground up.

TRADING PLACES

If you really want to establish a culture with empathy, have people switch jobs for a day or even a week so they can understand what other people have to go through.

Everyone benefits from the job switch. People have the opportunity to meet others they may not normally come into contact with during their working day. They exchange ideas on how to tackle challenges and form cross-company bonds that reinforce company values.

In the process, you have the opportunity to meet and impress managers who have the power to bring you onto their team. Make yourself memorable for your skill and affability. And it certainly makes sense for the company executives to work in various positions in other departments every once in a while. One cruise, all the senior officers, including the Captain, served Thanksgiving dinner to the crew, and it was a big hit.

SHIP TO SHORE

The lessons from these stories can easily be applied in a land-based or virtual business, no matter where you are in your career today or where you want to go. Here's how:

- One introduction, one referral, one sale can change the course of your entire life. Seek out opportunities wherever you go.
- One bourbon, one shot, and one beer can also be helpful in business when you... no, wait, that's if you're applying for a gig with George Thorogood. Forget I said anything.
- Make the best impression in the job you have today. Your performance may be judged for possible advancement. You never know who is watching.
- Opportunity presents itself in ways you could never foresee. Your path may not look exactly the way you envisioned it, but a redirect may be just the adventure you were looking for!
- Recognize the challenges of others and show appreciation for the job they do. You never know what someone else may be going through.
- Express your interest in learning and advancing to other positions. People aren't mind readers. Show your enthusiasm for wanting to better yourself and the people around you.

CHAPTER 5:

LOOSE LIPS SINK SHIPS: THE IMPACT OF GOSSIP

"LOOSE LIPS SINK SHIPS" is an idiom coined by the U.S government office of the War Advertising Council during World War II. The phrase featured prominently on posters distributed by the United States Office of War Information. Each soldier was issued a document that outlined rules of conduct before entering battle and included, "...your lips must remain sealed and your written hand must be guided by self-imposed censorship. This takes guts. Have you got them, or do you want your buddies and your country to pay the price for your showing off?"

The "Loose Lips" message was spread in film, too. The Bureau of Motion Pictures was formed to work with Hollywood movie production companies to make sure the public saw the message of war support. Newsreels and films were made in conjunction with Hollywood studios and shown to theater audiences at home, rallying support for the troops and driving home the message of keeping one's lips sealed. Soldiers weren't the only ones with access to critical military information. The war was fought on the home front too, with factory production of aircraft, parachutes, ammunition, and clothing.

Even in the private sector, words have tremendous power to damage an individual, a department, and even an entire company. Gossip can kill any business or office comradery. It can severely impact the work environment.

We've all witnessed office gossip, and some of us may have

unfortunately been the subject of it. You can imagine how the opportunities for gossip are magnified on board a ship. You take a dose of intrigue, add some liquor, people living in close quarters, visitors from all walks of life, and presto … innuendo can spread like wildfire.

As a manager, you need to prepare for the personnel issues that may arise from rumor. As an employee, you can do your part to prevent or mitigate careless words from causing harm.

"Whoever gossips to you will gossip about you."
—Spanish Proverb

We learn early on there is no privacy on a ship. We live together and eat together and play together and everybody knows everybody's business. Even in land-based businesses, some people spend more waking hours with their co-workers than their own families. You've heard the term work wife? Co-workers develop very deep and lasting relationships with each other. And like the old saying goes, "familiarity breeds contempt." Someone once told me, "If they don't know your business, they'll make it up." Unfortunately, that is sad but true.

GOSSIP AND RUMORS: TWO SIDES OF THE SAME TREACHEROUS COIN

Although it can be hard to write and regulate a policy regarding gossip, it is certainly worthwhile to address the dangers when onboarding new hires. It doesn't hurt to give occasional reminders at staff meetings either. Gossip is unprofessional, and rumors repeated frequently enough begin to gain credibility no matter how false or outrageous they may be. Trust me, if you share a picture of aliens operating car washes enough times, people will start to believe they are snatching bodies out of vehicles during the dry cycle and replacing them with cyborgs.

Rumors can be painful for the subject and reduce overall productivity as well.

If you have ever been on a cruise, you know there are dozens of performers, putting on spectacular shows for your entertainment. One of the highlights of my job over the years is I get to work with some incredibly talented people from all over the world. These individual entertainers have performed on some of the biggest stages in the world, from Las Vegas to Broadway to London's West End. I envy all of them because I am not an entertainer. I can tell a joke or two and host a big event or activity, but I can't carry a tune and you'll never catch me in tap shoes.

We also have production casts on board, with singers and dancers (and in later years, aerialists) who come on as a group for up to six or seven months at a time. They usually perform two large scale production shows per cruise in the main theater, and our guests love them. In the early years, there were anywhere from eight to twelve performers in the production cast, but in later years, as the ships got bigger, and the stages got bigger, the casts got bigger as well. I was on one ship with twenty-nine people in the cast. That is a big cast. A lot of people with a lot of different personalities and backgrounds and egos thrown in. (What? Performers have egos? C'mon. To be honest, anyone who gets on a stage to perform has to have a little bit of an ego, and that's a good thing.) It was never a dull moment with our casts. One Captain called us the "Drama Division," as there was always some sort of drama going on.

Over my career I have worked with well over a hundred production casts. And I want to say from the outset that ninety-eight percent—no, make that ninety-nine percent—of the casts I have worked with were some of the nicest, most talented, low-maintenance people I have ever met or worked with. We like low maintenance. Low maintenance is good. Low maintenance means you are professional, you do your job, stay out of trouble, and cause me very little stress. Cruise Directors like as little stress as possible. Again, ninety-nine percent of the casts were wonderful.

But oh that other one percent. They made up for the rest of

the casts ten times over. Just a group of people, or more exactly a few individuals within that group, who didn't get along for whatever reason. And since they were miserable, they were going to make everyone else miserable.

DRAMA, DRAMA, DRAMA

It all started with the offhand comment, "Oh, she's crazy." From there, it snowballed into an international incident.

There was a situation a number of years ago that had one-half of the cast butting heads with the other half. The drama began during rehearsals in a land-based studio before they even got to the ship. Personalities clashed.

Most of the people in the cast are in their twenties and thirties, but some of these kids are right out of high school. They're eighteen, nineteen years old and have brought the schoolyard inexperience and immaturity with them. For many, it is the first time away from home or away from their parents.

This particular cast was rehearsing for a full-blown Las Vegas style revue, complete with elaborate choreography, massive feather headpieces, and glittery costumes. To pull off such a production, rehearsals are quite intense.

Tiffany, age nineteen, was from Ohio, and had studied dance since childhood and was very excited to land a position in the cast. Life was one big party for Tiffany, who thought working on a cruise ship was like hitting the jackpot the first time you played the lottery.

Jessica, age twenty-seven, also had been training since childhood. Growing up in England with access to a wide variety of teachers and schools, Jessica had studied voice and classical ballet through college. Although getting a job on a ship was not her first choice, having not landed a spot in any major productions in the city, she was nevertheless quite serious about her role in the ship's production.

Tiffany would roll out of bed with a couple of hours sleep, after taking advantage of the city's nightlife, and race to rehearsal. On the other hand, Jessica practiced her voice and dance warm-ups for at least an hour before arriving at the studio—two women with different approaches to the same career.

One day the production schedule was altered, and rehearsals would not begin until the afternoon. Tiffany managed to arrive at rehearsal 10 minutes prior to start time when she happened upon Jessica, alone, in an empty hallway, preparing.

Being a practical young woman, Jessica had decided to combine her voice warm-ups with her dance warm-ups, without much thought to how this may appear to others. After all, there are as many ways to practice and prepare as there are artists to perform.

Tiffany could hear Jessica before she even turned the corner.

"Yingata yingata yingata. Rrrrrrruffles have rrrrrrridges. Rrrrrrrruffffles have rrrrridges."

Thump. Thump. Thump.

Followed by, "Bbbbbbbbbbb," rubber-lipped raspberry boat noises going up and down the scale.

Thump. Thump. Thump.

"Zzzzzzz. Zzzzzzz. Zzzzzzz."

While this may all look a little funny in print, these sounds are pretty common practice for singers to relax the jaw and activate the vocal folds.

Tiffany turned the corner as Jessica was launching into some classical ballet pliés and sautés. Knees out, heels together, arms outstretched, hands relaxed—aaaaand jump!—and at that moment, Jessica appeared like a colorful, exploding mushroom, shooting up out of the forest floor making motorboat and bee sounds.

Having studied dance but not voice, Tiffany had no context for what she witnessed and found this scene to be hilarious. She couldn't wait to share what she had seen with the other dancers, and with not just a little derision, she added the opinion, "Jessica is absolutely crazy." Not missing an opportunity to describe the scene to other cast members, all references to Jessica were subsequently "Crazy Jessica."

As you can imagine, it did not take long for the gossip to reach Jessica's ears. Not everyone who heard Tiffany's story thought it was an unreasonable practice and assumed Tiffany was (a) considerably less experienced, and (b) ever so slightly jealous of the red-haired Jessica, with the bigger role in the Vegas production.

By the time Jessica came across Tiffany and a couple of her friends in the hall, she was red hot. Not being the shrinking violet type, Jessica leveled her gaze at Tiffany and hissed, "I hear you're going around telling everybody I'm crazy. Really? You think I'm crazy? Wait till we get on board the ship; then you'll see how crazy I really am." Theater people *can* be dramatic.

Many cruise lines, corporations, and government agencies have a policy called "See something, say something" with regard to concerns about health and safety. For example, if you see a suspicious package at the airport left on its own, you should report it to an airport employee. Likewise, if you are working on a ship and you feel somebody is destructive or might hurt themselves or might cause harm to another person, you're supposed to say something, report it to a manager. For instance, if two crew members are in a room and one says, "I don't know if I can take this anymore. This job is killing me," or "If I weren't here, nobody would know the difference," then this is definitely behavior that needs to be reported to a manager or supervisor.

Tiffany used the "See something, say something" policy as an excuse to go to the director and basically tell on Jessica for confronting her in the hallway, citing Jessica's words as a threat and evidence that she really *was* crazy.

The director then went to Jessica and said simply, "Tiffany says you're crazy," and took no further action.

As human nature would have it, factions developed. Cast members chose sides. There was Team Jessica and Team Tiffany.

These two groups had become the Sharks and the Jets of the cruise line. Queue the *West Side Story* music.

Team Tiffany was now quite a bit larger than the few individuals who made the initial statement to the director. And from there, it just blew up. The two groups faced off.

One singer went to the director about another singer. Then a dancer filed an official complaint against another dancer claiming he was intentionally bumping into him on stage. Dancers all have their marks they have to hit. They know exactly, to the inch, where they're supposed to be at any given time, because that's what rehearsals are for. There are numbers across the entire stage so that dancers know where they're supposed to be on point—stage left, downstage, or upstage, and sometimes they pass extremely close to each other. Sometimes they intertwine with each other in dance routines. We record all of these shows. We even record the rehearsals. Because of the behavior and complaints, we had to go back and spend hours looking at the show reels to see what happened and resolve the situation.

The tension continued to escalate. It got so bad that one guy from Team Jessica was walking down the street in port, while cast members from Team Tiffany were walking the other way. The guy went to management and said, "They were pointing at me and laughing at me. They were making fun of me. This is a hostile work environment. I can't work under these conditions."

Unfortunately, I arrived on board in the middle of this crisis, about three months in, which was already in full-blown "crazy" mode. Because it had escalated so far, I let the experts handle it, as they were already involved, including the Captain, Staff Captain, the Human Resources Manager and Hotel Director. When it gets that high up, you know there's a problem.

This behavior continued to escalate through the entire six-month contract. HR shoreside and corporate attorneys from the head office got involved because people were threatening to sue for mental anguish.

Two people claimed it was a hostile workplace environment. People from the head office production facilities had to fly out to the ship to meet with the cast because it got so bad. Everybody had to prepare written statements and be interviewed. One of the main targets left the ship and had to be paid for the remainder of her contract.

Because one inexperienced person witnessed something she did not understand and chose to gossip, dozens of people became involved, hundreds of hours were spent investigating, and thousands of dollars were paid to attorneys to rectify the situation.

All of this hullabaloo was because rumors started and gossip spread. This out-of-control situation could have been avoided if it was handled immediately and properly.

NIP IT

I've got five words of serious advice that I guarantee you can avoid a situation like this one from spiraling out of control. To quote Barney Fife from *The Andy Griffith Show*, "Nip it in the bud."

The director should have immediately turned the problem over to HR, who could have brought everyone in the same room to share their side of the story and mediate a resolution. Resolve it then and there or don't board the ship.

As a team member, you should always remain professional. Don't engage in gossip. Remember that anything you say can be taken out of context and repeated. Some words said blithely can take on very serious meanings, such as "crazy," "stupid," and "sick."

Don't jump to conclusions about things you see. For example, on cruise ships, if people are in the crew bar at night after work and they see a guy and a girl sitting and talking together, ooh, all of a sudden, they're dating and all of a sudden they're sleeping together. And all of a sudden this and all of a sudden that. Or, God forbid, the worst thing is that if a guy and a girl leave the crew bar together, even if they're just going to their own cabins, the look of it is enough to start rumors.

Nip it in the bud. Plan for the worst instincts of people; don't assume maturity. The people involved in the "crazy girl" story did not have the experience that would have taught them how to handle situations like that. NIP IT IN THE BUD. These dramas hurt everyone and can ruin a company's culture.

When uncomfortable and potentially litigious situations arise, get everyone in the same room and DISCUSS. Communication is everything. Tell them, "We are going to stay here until it's sorted out. We aren't paid to be friends, but we are paid to be professional and we will resolve this issue." Get proactive about allowing people to speak. As a leader, you should communicate what you need and open lines of dialogue. Use your resources (HR departments).

The guiding principle behind your training and policies should be to create a mentally healthy workplace people will look forward to coming to every day. Research shows that people who are happy and satisfied at work are actually healthier than their miserable counterparts. According to *Forbes*, the average U.S. worker will spend 90,000 hours of their lifetime at work, and they didn't even take into account the cruise industry! Workplace stress has been linked to health problems and on-the-job accidents.

When people feel appreciated and safe at their workplace, they are happier and more engaged. According to PositivePsychology. com, "Organizations with higher levels of employee engagement indicated lower business costs, improved performance outcomes, lower staff turnover and absenteeism, and fewer safety incidents (Gallup, 2015)."

The cruise industry is my happy place. It has kept me excited about getting up in the morning, greeting and working with the crew, meeting the passengers, and learning something new every day. Take my four decades of experience and some of my stories and put them to work for your business. The lessons in this chapter can save you stress, heartache, and most importantly, the money you would spend defending a lawsuit.

SHIP TO SHORE

The lessons from these stories can easily be applied in a land-based or virtual business. Here's how:

- Never underestimate a situation's ability to spiral out of control when it's not handled promptly.
- Fix potential problems immediately to avoid unexpected and unnecessary consequences.
- Make your work environment a place where employees feel comfortable coming to you with problems BEFORE they escalate.
- If the shoe was on the other foot, how would you feel if someone said the same thing about you?
- If you hear a rumor about someone and your first thought is, "Really? I would never have expected that," then trust your instinct. If you hear a comment about a person you have known for years that is completely contrary to the behavior you have witnessed, consider it a rumor. (Unless, of course, it's about Judy in accounting. We all know she's nuts.)
- Whether you are owner, manager, or staff, you can set an example for others by refraining from the type of talk that hurts. Lead by example by not tolerating gossip in conversation.

"One person's crazy is another person's reasonable."
—Anonymous

One of the very talented (stress-free) production casts.

CHAPTER 6:

THROW OFF THE BOWLINES

"Twenty years from now you will be more disappointed by the things you didn't do than by the ones you did. So, throw off the bowline. Sail away from the safe harbor. Catch the trade winds in your sails. Explore. Dream. Discover."
—Mark Twain

THAT QUOTE IS PARTICULARLY APPROPRIATE to my lifelong experience with the cruise industry. Where would my life be if I hadn't accepted Mr. Ziplow's offer to sail away from the safe harbor of Fort Lauderdale? It is doubtful that a teaching career would have taken me around the world, introduced me to Broadway stars as well as the wonderful woman I worked with on board who would become my wife. I wouldn't be enjoying gourmet meals prepared by renowned chefs or going to work in a billion-dollar floating office.

I accepted that first offer, and the subsequent opportunities, largely based on my faith that I could do the job—or *learn* how to do the job. And remembering that second part—learning—is key to success. When you take on a new position, you will not know every nuance of how to perform that job fully or correctly.

I've worked with ten cruise lines over the years. (Some of them are gone now, but not because of me, I promise.) By the time I became an Assistant Cruise Director, I had worked on almost twenty different ships. I started in the casino as a cashier and worked as a port lecturer before joining the Cruise Division on my way up the ladder to Cruise Director.

In every position I held, I made it a point to get to know the people around me. Building relationships is key to a great work environment and increases your fulfillment and opportunities. Automatic raises and promotions don't come your way for just showing up. Not only have I befriended the people around me, I have also stayed in touch with many of them for thirty years. Not a week passes when I am not in touch with someone from the industry, no matter where we have moved or gone in our careers.

I had been trying to get hired as cruise staff for a while with Royal Caribbean. I knew the hiring manager, Dave, and had been calling him from time to time. Every time, he would reply, "Nope, don't have anything." "Still nothing." "Not yet. I'll let you know." To his credit, he always took my calls.

Finally, in February 1991, he called, and said, "Okay, I have a cruise staff position for you. I need you next week on either the *Emerald Seas* or the *Song of America*." *Song of America* was a fairly new ship. Everybody loved it. It got great reviews and was well-known in the industry. The *Emerald Seas* was a lot smaller, a lot older and running three- and four-day cruises.

In the cruise industry, starting a new job the following week happens quite often, as they need you right away. Somebody got fired. Somebody quit. "I need you tomorrow" is a common thing to hear, which is why we always need to have our documents up to date—physicals, paperwork, passports—everything in order, because you never know when you're going to get the call.

When the dust settled, I wound up as cruise staff on *The Emerald Seas* out of Fort Lauderdale, Florida. And it worked out great. The Cruise Director, Bill, was a wonderful guy and is still with the company. I was determined to rise through the ranks.

Two months later, I was promoted to Assistant Cruise Director on the biggest ship in the world, *The Sovereign of the Seas*. To go from cruise staff to Assistant Cruise Director on the largest ship in the world in two months was crazy fast. This was May of 1991; I was thirty-six at the time. Admittedly, I really had doubts, because when I first joined the ship, I thought, *Holy crap, what am I getting myself into? This is the biggest ship in the world, and I'm the Assistant Cruise Director.*

I worked hard and tried to learn as much as I could. My philosophy was: "Do the work now; you can relax and go ashore later." Otherwise, that work just hangs over your head.

We received great ratings and I worked for the top Cruise Directors in the fleet, learning as much as possible. Because again, this was the flagship, and only the most senior Cruise Directors were selected to work on board. All of them were my mentors, people that I watched very closely, picking and choosing what to emulate. *Okay, I'll need to do that. Oh, I don't want to do that. Oh yes. I like the way he does that.* I learned a lot from each one of them. Special thanks to Ray, Jim and Jeff.

MOVING ON UP

In December of 1991, a Cruise Director was set to replace the one leaving for vacation. The procedure is called a "handover;" they'll both sail together for a week. This way the replacement sees the operation and knows what's happening. The new guy came on board and sailed for a week with the Cruise Director to learn the ropes on the *Sovereign*, as he had never sailed on that class of ship. I worked with them for the transition and introduced the new CD to the whole team.

It was the end of the cruise and we had just returned to port. We usually docked around six or seven in the morning, as the semi-trailers arrive with the food and provisions for the next cruise, which is all loaded into the bowels of the ship for the next voyage.

The logistics are crazy. In a matter of hours, 2,500 people (and with the newer, bigger ships, over 6,000 people) debark, the ship is prepped and cleaned, and 2,500 new people embark. Could land-based hotels accomplish this massive undertaking? I don't think so.

That morning, the new Cruise Director was supposed to take over, but instead, he packed his bags and walked off the ship.

Record scratches. Crowd goes silent. He did what?

He just walked off and went home. We had never experienced anything like this before. He was quitting on the spot.

He just said, "Nobody told me it was going to be like this."

All hands on deck, we are going down.

The Cruise Director who was going on vacation that day had to stay an extra week, and trust me, he was not happy. It may be common to sign somebody up for the next week, but impossible to fill a position within hours. The next week was crazy. Who was available? This was late December, right around Christmas when most people want to be home with their families. Management brought several Cruise Directors back to fill in temporarily until they could find a permanent replacement.

As all of this was going on, unbeknownst to me, some of the members of the Cruise Division, including the senior managers, went to the head office and lobbied on my behalf, saying, "Let Paul do it. He's ready to take over as the Cruise Director." Now this was December, and I had been the assistant since May. I had already done two contracts on board, and had established some great relationships. They kept saying, "Just give it to Paul, he'll do a great job."

On Saturday, I went over to the head office and met with Peter Compton, the Vice President of Entertainment, whom I had known for quite some time. Finally, he said, "Okay, are you ready to do this?" And the next week I was a permanent Cruise Director.

In truth, there were other people within the company who had been assistant longer than me. And believe me, I'm sure they felt they were better qualified, and that might have been true, but they were on other ships and I was right there. I already knew the ship and had built relationships with many key people on board. Timing is everything, and you have to take advantage of it when those things come your way.

As a leader, I make and maintain friendships at every level of the organization. The first people I get to know are the people who to me are the most important. We call them the foundation of the division, because without them, nothing works. In our division they're called the stage staff, the tech staff, or the "black shirts," because that's what they wore. They do the heavy lifting for the entire entertainment division, from back stage set-ups to loading and unloading sound and light equipment and troubleshooting technical issues. They are our unsung heroes and get none of the glory, but without them, nothing happens. So of course you want to get on their good side, learn their names, and treat them with respect. That's all anyone wants in this world, is to be treated with respect.

I had been really nervous about taking on the Assistant Cruise Director position, because I thought of all the work involved: There was so much administrative and back-of-house paperwork that was new to me, as well as the scheduling and hosting of many activities on the largest ship in the world. But, I decided to ride the wave I was given and threw off the bowlines. By the time the Cruise Director position needed to be filled, I had the confidence to accept the job.

THERE'S ALWAYS ONE

There was only one person who wasn't thrilled with the decision for me to be promoted to Cruise Director: my boss on board. As the Hotel Director, he let me know from the beginning that he did not agree with the decision to promote me and said so in no uncertain terms: "I don't agree with this decision. I'll support you, but I don't think you should be Cruise Director on the *Sovereign* as your first ship. You need to start on a smaller ship and work your way up, and I'm not happy about it. You need to know that."

The Hotel Director, who went by the nickname Bud, was very well-known around the fleet for being very good at his job, as well as for his love of a good time, which was evident in the way he expected some of us, including me, to have a beer with him every day at lunch. He was the boss, so we would dutifully meet out on deck at the pool bar to have one beer—to his four or five. (He jokingly called it "quality control inspection.") The rest of us had to get back to work, but the boss would head back to his cabin.

INTERNATIONAL NAPTIME

There's something in the cruise industry called "international naptime." That's the time from approximately noon until three in the afternoon when many officers will go on break, grab some lunch, and then have a few hours to rest and relax before their afternoon shift. And you don't bother them, unless there's an emergency. Emergencies include man overboard and icebergs. That's it.

You don't disturb any of the officers, but on some of the ships, the theater is right under the cabins of the Captain, Staff Captain, and Chief Engineer. These senior officers are up early and work hard. This block of time is so paramount that observing it dictated to us when we could run rehearsals in the theater. I had to start and stop rehearsals around the international naptime schedule. There was more than one senior officer who called down to say, "If you don't shut that music off, I'm going to have the Chief Electrician come down and rip the wiring right out of the wall!" They had no concern at all that we had a performance to rehearse for that night. Again, these were just a few of the senior officers; most of them were wonderful and fully understanding (just in case I work with them again!)

On one ship, our shows on formal nights ran at 8:30 p.m. and then again at 10:30 p.m. So our 10:30 show ended around 11:30 p.m. If we were changing time zones, which we usually do, the clock would go ahead an hour as we were headed to the Eastern Caribbean, so now it was 12:30 a.m., which means I'm keeping the Captain, the Chief Engineer, and other senior officers awake until that time.

These officers were not especially happy with me. This is a state-of-the-art Broadway theater, with speakers located in the ceiling as well as ground level, and in the house, the main speakers are suspended from the ceiling. We actually had to take the speakers down, put in insulation and padding, and then put the speakers back up to help muffle the sound. I understood because these Captains coming into port the next day sometimes have to be up at four or five in the morning in order to take the ship into the channels or the port where they dock early in the morning. I understood their position, but I couldn't plan earlier shows due to time conflicts with dinners and specially planned formal night events.

THIS BUD'S FOR YOU

The Hotel Director hosted his own table in the dining room, and Bud, being the sociable guy he was, would always invite people to his table; the Food and Beverage Director and I were expected to eat with him every night. This meant I had to have dinner every night with a guy who didn't think I was doing a really good job. The Food and Beverage Director would always sit between us and run interference. *Oh, so you think I'm incompetent, great, pass the rolls.*

Over time, Bud saw that I knew what I was doing. He saw me on stage and hosting events. The ratings were excellent. The revenue that was coming from my heavy promotion of Bingo games, shore excursions and the casino was very good. I was ticking off all the boxes, and he still didn't give me the best evaluation. The first time he gave me sort of an average one. My bonus was based on my evaluation—the higher my evaluation, the higher my bonus, part of his strategy, I'm sure. Just doing my job was not going to be enough. Even though I had confidence in my performance, I went a step further and made efforts to include him. If I had a big problem, I would go to Bud and say, "I need your advice on something. What do you think I should do?" And of course, he loved that. Who doesn't love people coming to them, asking for advice? Despite his attitude toward me, I did maintain respect for his position.

After about six months, we were sitting around the dinner table one evening, well into the third bottle of wine. Then Bud ordered after dinner drinks all around—B-52s. I don't know if you've ever had one, but they are a layered shot of coffee liquor, Baileys Irish Cream, and Grand Marnier. After the third round, Bud leaned back in his chair, around the Food and Beverage Manager, and told me, "You know, I doubted you at the beginning, but you really came through. Congratulations." Which sounded really more like "Congrooshalooshins."

I continued to maintain a good rapport with Bud. He was a big guy and I got him involved in exercise and eating healthier. But trust me, we never did end up really good friends. I just kept my head down and knew I could do the job, and Bud and I worked together for several contracts without any problems. It was just tough at the beginning when everybody else supported me except my big boss. But it worked out in the end, and I've always treasured the "congrooshalooshins."

WHAT ABOUT YOU?

How many times have you thought to yourself, *I could do that job*? Well, there's a very good chance you can. Be honest with yourself, though. Are you saying that because you want the job for the higher pay, the perks, or the prestige? Do you think you deserve it because of how long you've been with the company? Or, do you think you have the knowledge or potential to do that job really well?

If you answered, "because I have the ability," then set your sights on that job and make a plan. Start with doing your current job to the best of your abilities. We've all seen those people at work, who look like they are bored with their jobs, or who aren't taking their responsibilities very seriously. Don't be one of them.

The effort isn't over once you've gotten the new job, either, as you can see from my story. It's not all smooth sailing just because you convinced someone to give you the job. You lobbied for promotion, and next you need to master it and broadcast your efficiency to others.

Don't listen to other voices, like Bud, who did not believe in me. Believe in yourself and in what you're doing and know that you're right for the job. I'm glad I did.

Sometimes a person's biggest struggle is overcoming the negative voices around them. Only listen to your own, so make sure it's positive.

SHIP TO SHORE

The lessons from these stories can easily be applied in a land-based or virtual business. Here's how:

- Make friends. You know what they say, you spend more time with your coworkers than your family, so you might as well get to know them.
- Offer an olive branch. Be the one to reach out. Do you think you got off on the wrong foot with someone? Talk it out. They might be feeling the same way about you.
- If you're at dinner with someone who thinks you're incompetent and can't locate an olive branch, offer some Olive Oil. It can work just as well. In a pinch, offer Crisco.
- Respect the position. No matter what job you have, even if you feel it is menial, it is someone else's dream job. Appreciate it for what it provides you today and where it can take you tomorrow.
- Endorse your coworkers. Be a cheerleader. Give other people credit and share their achievements.
- Legendary UCLA basketball coach John Wooden said, "A strong leader accepts blame and gives credit. A weak leader gives blame and accepts the credit." Be a strong leader.

CHAPTER 7:

ROCKING THE BOAT: EFFECTIVELY HANDLE CONFLICT

CONFLICT ISN'T UNCOMFORTABLE for everyone. There are those who embrace it, churn it, and feed on dragging others into it. We can't go through our careers hoping to avoid uncomfortable situations, especially in management. Everyone in supervisory roles should be trained in management conflict before they step into the work arena. Policies should be clearly written in employee manuals.

I have seen some doozies living and working in close quarters with thousands of people over the past forty years. There are policies in place to help guide the process, but my greatest training in conflict resolution has come from experience. A very minor incident of no real consequence can snowball into disaster. For instance, who would think Bingo could cause an uproar, ending in fistfights and blood on the carpet?

We were taking a two-week Christmas cruise from San Juan, Puerto Rico, through the Panama Canal, and ending up in Acapulco, Mexico. The Christmas cruise is always one of our most popular and people book it up to a year in advance. Because it's a holiday, there are more children aboard than usual. On this particular cruise, out of 2,000 guests, 700 of them were children, more than a third of the ship.

Now this cruise happened in the mid-nineties, before a lot of the technology was developed we are using today. There were a number of wealthy families on board. The type of family that employs a nanny for their children. I guess they must have given the nannies time off for the holiday, because none of these families brought their nannies along with them—as was evident by the number of unsupervised children roaming free throughout the ship. And I'm not talking just during the day, running around the pool. Where is Mary Poppins when you need her?

These children were running up and down the halls all through the night, in roving packs of three or more. Not only was the sound of giggling, squealing, and thundering footsteps a nuisance, the behavior got totally out of hand. They switched the room service orders left on the doorknobs for the next morning's breakfast. They removed the Do Not Disturb door hangers and switched them to Make Up the Room, so stateroom attendants were walking in on guests in all forms of undress. They were even knocking on doors at one in the morning. Despite making several announcements regarding the unsuitability of unsupervised youngsters, the behavior persisted. Yes, there is security on board patrolling the ship, but they can't be everywhere all the time.

Needless to say, there were quite a few visits to the Guest Services desk about these little hellions. "Why didn't you tell me there would be so many children on board?" was one of the more frequent questions. Parents tend to keep their children with them at Christmas. Childless passenger suggestions ranged from locking kids in their rooms to some more unsuitable things that involved high dives and milk cartons.

The ship quickly divided into two social camps. Those with children and those without passed each other in the hallway with dirty looks and grumbles. And another dynamic came into play: those guests from the United States, and those who were not. Even the people with well-behaved children were concerned about being identified with the other families. The families with the worst-behaved children, unsurprisingly, felt that ship policies didn't apply to them at all. Some of the adults were not much better. Many of the fathers insisted on smoking cigars in the dining room and other unapproved areas, ironically wondering why these kids were incapable of following the rules.

WORLD WRESTLING BINGO?

Despite the crew trying to uphold policies, clean up ashes, and smooth ruffled feathers, tensions among the passengers were running high by the end of the cruise. Everything came to a head in an incident we now refer to as the Bloody Bingo Battle.

Bingo was a very popular multi-day event, with the final jackpot bingo game rising to as much as $20,000. This was nothing to sneeze at and people were getting excited. Games were held in the main theater, which was quickly getting packed on the final day of the cruise.

One of the grandmothers (at this point, notorious as a lax disciplinarian and supplier of endless sticky treats) arrived at the theater as soon as the doors opened and proceeded to hold seats in the second row for her family—her entire extended family of fifteen. Grandma placed her handbag on one seat, and her sweater on another seat at the end of the row.

We had a "no-saving-seats" policy, and the Assistant Cruise Director, Mary Grace, walked over and quietly mentioned this to Grandma, who completely ignored her. Instead, Grandma stood, with her back to the stage, facing the doors at the rear of the theater, scanning for her family. Whenever she would see a family member, she would wave her arms wildly and yell their name. "Tina! Tina! Tina! Maria! Maria! Maria! Here. Down here. I saved you a seat." Grandma was not easy to miss in her yellow and orange caftan and surprisingly booming voice. Her family did not acknowledge her entreaties with much urgency and continued on with their conversations instead of heading down the aisle to join her.

By this point, the theater was near capacity and several people had gone to Mary Grace to complain about Grandma and the empty seats. Mary Grace reassured people she was taking their complaints seriously and would do her best to address them. Then she alerted security to the increased tension in the theater.

A few brave souls decided to ignore Grandma and sit in the saved seats anyway, as there were almost none left elsewhere. Her volume rose even more as she yelled at the interlopers and waved her billowy sleeves for emphasis.

By this point, Grandma was in the middle of the aisle, raising her fist at a large, bearded guest. Her son and son-in-law arrived and began squeezing into the row to join her and started yelling at Bearded Guy. Bearded Guy's wife walked up behind him to add her two cents-worth to the argument, and as Bearded Guy turned to look at his wife, he bumped into Grandma.

It really was a tiny little bump, and an accident. However, Bearded Guy's elbow clipped Grandma right between the shoulder blades. She lurched forward and as she did, launched her dentures into the next row. And although the woman seated there had been watching this entire drama unfold, she was completely unprepared to have Grandma's dentures land in her lap. Her response was to jump up and scream, and as she did, the dentures slid off her lap to the floor. Grandma screamed. Thinking Bearded Guy had assaulted Grandma, the sons started pummeling Bearded Guy. In a move never before witnessed in a wrestling ring, Bearded Guy's wife climbed over him and threw herself on the back of one of the sons, like a game of chicken in the pool, and landed a solid right hook into the other son.

Security intervened, broke up the melee, and remained in the theater for the duration of that day's Bingo game.

Some blood was shed.

The dentures were found.

No lawsuits were filed, most likely because the son didn't want to admit that an Ohio housewife got the best of him.

Really, could you make this ship up?

BINGO BRAWL... LESSONS LEARNED

What seems inconsequential to you can be very serious for someone else.

Conflict is emotional. Not logical.

Know when to handle a situation yourself, when it is time to "kick it up" the chain of command, or hand it off for another type of intervention.

People are serious about their Bingo.

Another thing to consider are the optics. Everything winds up on social media. You will be watched and documented, so slow down and think about your actions and your language. Don't allow the emotions of others to change your vocabulary. Many workplaces have closed circuit interior security cameras. Instead of thinking of them as an intrusion, think of them as your eyewitnesses. A camera can be witness to both innocence and guilt.

There used to be a travel promotion that went, "What happens in Vegas, stays in Vegas." Well, we changed it up a bit to read, "What happens on a ship, ends up on YouTube."

FORK IT OVER

Presenting dinner on board a cruise ship is like a cross between a Hollywood production and a military maneuver. Meals are beautifully presented, and the process is highly regimented so that all meals are served with the same superior quality every time on every ship.

This means that one hour prior to a meal, every server is in the dining room, spreading the tablecloths, folding the napkins, adding the flowers, and arranging the silverware to perfection. Every table, every place setting must be Instagram worthy. The dining room manager takes one last look before opening the doors.

When friction started to develop between two of the wait staff,

Julian, the manager, had to nip it in the bud before the tension became noticeable to the passengers.

We recognize the need to be sensitive to different countries and different cultures, but the following incident caught a few of us off guard when we witnessed a culture clash between two men from Spain. We might assume that two young men, meeting so far from home, would bond over their similarities, but these two circled each other like wary street dogs. The cause for their onboard clashes? Football. In Spain, the club you support can be an indicator of not just your locale, but your political beliefs, as well.

Pedro, suave with the guests and flamboyant in his personal interactions with cruise staff, was team FC Barcelona. "Mes que un club," more than a club, since the Spanish Civil War, FC Barcelona has been the choice for left-leaning progressives throughout Spain.

Hernando, conservative and stoic both personally and professionally, grew up two hours outside of Madrid in Avila, famous for its cobblestone streets and ancient walls. He, of course, supported Real Madrid.

The two were overheard on numerous occasions arguing over the famous Luís Figo switch from FC Barcelona to Real Madrid. Having once been a fan favorite in Barcelona, fans became so enraged over Figo's switch to Madrid, that yelling and jeering did not satisfy their anger. At one match, someone in the crowd hurled a pig's head onto the pitch just as Figo was preparing to take a corner for Real.

I've always wondered how that guy got a pig's head through security. It's not exactly like sneaking popcorn into the movies. A severed pig's head weighs nearly 20 pounds.

Anyway, back to the story. One day, Hernando went to Julian, his supervisor and dining room manager, and complained that Pedro had been trying to make him look bad. He said that after the dining room was all prepped, Pedro would slip through and steal the silverware off the tables in the section where Hernando worked. Once the meal started, diner after diner would wave Hernando over to ask for forks and knives, keeping him busier than he needed to be, and making the cruise line look unprofessional.

Julian decided to bring Pedro in to hear his side of the story. Hernando was present as well and the two men faced off, each fidgeting behind a chair in the office. Pedro flatly refused the allegations and Hernando became even more agitated. Julian knew he had an ace up his sleeve. "You know gentlemen, we can resolve this quite easily. I can call up the CCTV footage from the dining room."

With that, Pedro began sputtering, and defending himself by saying it was all just a big joke. "That may be, but when the shenanigans are noticeable to the passengers, it's a matter of the company's reputation," reminded Julian, making it clear that jobs were at stake. The brief chastisement was all it took to get these two young men focused on keeping their jobs and putting their rivalries aside (at least in public). Julian didn't even have to go look for the footage.

HANDLING CONFLICT INVOLVES MORE EQ THAN IQ

IQ only accounts for about twenty percent of what makes a person successful. EQ, our emotional intelligence quotient, cannot be underestimated. It is a basic understanding of other humans and what makes them tick, and learning that skill starts with some very candid self-examination of our own motivations.

According to Mitrefinch.com, "Approximately eighty-two percent of global companies now utilize these tests for executive positions; seventy-two percent of these companies give the tests to middle management and only fifty-nine percent of companies give the tests to entry-level positions."

Developing EQ requires an understanding of emotions and how to regulate them. When faced with moderating a disagreement among team members, it is important to help them find common ground for resolution.

I highly recommend Psychologist Daniel Goleman's book, *Emotional Intelligence.* In it, he explains, "Leadership is not domination, but the art of persuading people to work toward a common goal."

SHIP TO SHORE

The lessons from these stories can easily be applied in a land-based or virtual business. Here's how:

- When conflict arises, facilitate mediation as quickly as possible.
- Maintain your objectivity. Don't take sides in a dispute. Your role as a leader is to facilitate a solution from all the parties involved in a conflict.
- Recognize everyone's need to be heard. Listening is a critical element of leadership. Just ask my wife, she's told me that a million times.
- Read up on EQ, recognize it, and use it to your advantage. You have to remember at the end of the day, you're dealing with people, not stats and facts.

CHAPTER 8:

ALL HANDS ON DECK: BUILDING EXCEPTIONAL TEAMS

IN MY ROLE AS CRUISE DIRECTOR, I am one of the most visible people on board the ship. The crew know me, and the guests all meet me in one way or another. It is my voice they hear on the PA system every day, making announcements. It is my face they see as they tune into the onboard morning TV show I host. It is me they see in the theater as Master of Ceremonies hosting the nightly entertainment. I am the liaison between the cruise line and their customers.

I am very careful how I conduct myself every minute of every day while I'm out in public, because I never know who's watching, and I want to make any interaction a positive experience. Naturally, I want to make a good impression on the guests to make their cruise enjoyable; I also want to leave the crew with a positive experience as well. Why should I be concerned with someone I outrank? Many of these junior officers have dreams of rising through the ranks and they consciously or unconsciously may be modeling my behavior. And they may outrank me one day. As the saying goes, "Be careful whose toes you step on today because they may be connected to the foot that kicks your ass tomorrow."

YOU NEVER KNOW WHO'S WATCHING

Think about the bosses you've had over the years. Did you copy techniques from one and reject behavior exhibited by another? Did you have a nasty boss who ruled by volume and intimidation? Many people have had that sort of spiteful boss and subconsciously learned that the way to the top is paved with bullying and favoritism. As we now know, companies are favoring EQ over IQ and will be looking for management candidates who can lead with empathy and compassion. Good leaders build good leaders, and that takes self-confidence.

At all times, act as if someone is watching you and taking notes. Treat customers, employees, bosses, and vendors all with the same courtesy and respect.

I'm a big sports fan, and one night I was watching a post-game interview with one of the players from the winning team, and he said something that really stuck with me. When asked who made the biggest difference in his life, he replied, "The people who made the biggest difference in my life never knew they made the biggest difference in my life." Wow, that was a telling statement.

Who, besides your parents, has made the biggest difference in your life? A teacher? A coach? A singing instructor? A boss? Do they even know what a big difference they made in your life? Probably not. And they'll likely never know unless you have an opportunity to tell them someday.

Could you be the person making a difference in someone else's life one day? Maybe you already have.

To become a good leader, to rise up the ladder, everyone needs to be their absolute best at what they are doing today. Otherwise, it's like saying, "I don't need to practice the scales to learn how to play the piano. I'll start practicing when I learn how to play Beethoven's sonatas." Every step builds to the next level. The lessons we learn in entry-level positions will serve us well as we achieve greater heights in our career—lessons like punctuality, attention to detail, and taking pride in our work.

I love mentoring people and watching them move up the corporate ladder. One of my greatest joys is watching people reach their potential and get to the position they dream about. I see a sports staff member who wants to be a Sports Manager, or a youth staff member who wants to become a Youth Manager. I see a cruise staff member who wants to become an Assistant Cruise Director, or even a Cruise Director. I love helping people get to where they want to go, and I'm not threatened by that. I hope I've been a positive influence in their journey.

LEADERS AREN'T NECESSARILY BOSSES

Some people love the position they are in and don't want to go higher. Not everyone dreams of promotion and extra responsibility. These people can be leaders, too. They set examples for new hires on how to conduct themselves and how to take pride in their work. They are the people their coworkers come to for advice. A good leader inspires, makes others feel accepted, and helps achieve group goals.

Part of being a good leader is recognizing the skills others bring to the table. You can learn from everyone.

My wife went to school to become a private investigator, and one of the things taught in that program is to utilize all of your resources. In other words, look around you and assess everything you can use for innovation. People are resources, too.

If you're in a crisis and need to take action right away, ask all of your employees, "Okay, we have an emergency. Have you ever experienced anything like this?" Everybody comes to the job with many life experiences we don't know about. The guy who just joined the company may, in a previous job, have had an experience that could help you now. So, I always say, never disregard anyone. Use all your resources.

SHIP TO SHORE

The lessons from these stories can be helpful to everyone on the job. Here's how:

- Model leadership behavior in whatever you do. You never know who is watching.
- You're not the only one who has the answers or has to come up with them. Be open to learning from everyone.
- Continue to learn and study. Read the biographies of business leaders you admire and take continuing education classes. Oscar Wilde once said, "You can never be overdressed or overeducated." Comedian Steven Wright once asked, "What's another word for Thesaurus?"

CHAPTER 9:

WALK THE PLANK: FIRE EFFECTIVELY

YOU'LL BE RELIEVED TO HEAR I've only had to make a handful of people walk the plank during my career. And they were all given fair warning and a soft blindfold.

In all seriousness though, have you ever seen a college course called Firing 101? Or an online continuing education seminar titled How to Can Somebody? Or maybe a weekend retreat called Getting Rid of that Dead Weight? There is little to no training for how to "let someone go," other than the employee handbook guidelines as to what constitutes the grounds for a dismissal. It is a horrible thing to be fired. It is also very uncomfortable to be the one doing the firing.

When it becomes evident that someone is not capable of fulfilling their duty, process and documentation are crucial for clear understanding and the avoidance of litigation. First and foremost, rules and expectations for behavior must be clearly stated from day one. Never assume that people will see eye-to-eye on what acceptable behavior is. Can you imagine someone walking into my office and saying, "Wadya mean, I'm not allowed to get drunk and dive naked into the swimming pool?"

The steps for disciplinary action and termination need to be clearly outlined in company documentation. They should also be verbally reviewed in your onboarding process.

The ninety-day probation period is an efficient test within any organization. This gives employer and employee a chance to get to know each other, understand expectations, blend with other employees and the company culture, and in the case of the cruise industry, make sure people are cut out for life at sea. It can be very glamorous, but some people feel restricted by the many rules and regulations. Ship life is not for everyone.

After the probation period, most cruise lines have a three-step process for removing someone from their position: The first infraction of the rules results in a disciplinary assessment. In other words, the offense is brought to the attention of senior management.

The second step is to offer verbal counseling to the crew member. This is a discussion to review the crew member's behavior and invite feedback. This conversation is a matter of record and stays in the crew member's file for a year.

Next, a total of three written warnings can be issued to a crew member for any number of violations. This third warning triggers a Master's Hearing. HR sets up a meeting with the Captain, which usually takes place in port.

One of the hardest decisions that Captains have to make concerns letting somebody go. Some people deserve to be fired right away, but there are some people with extenuating circumstances and sadly, it's a shame, but sometimes they have to be dismissed because they have broken the rules multiple times, and companies must be consistent and fair.

Expectations are clearly communicated to all employees from day one, and everyone knows there is a zero-tolerance policy for violations such as being drunk on the job, fighting, stealing, and harassment, amongst others.

FOLLOW THE PROCESS

Without a process in place, firing someone is incredibly challenging. Most people do not like confrontation. Whether it's an employee or a vendor, people want to avoid the awkward conversation and will put up with months or years of poor performance. The person getting fired wants to save their job. They want to negotiate and appeal to the supervisor on a personal level. "How can you fire me? You know I have a sick mother, a kid who needs shoes, and lots of bills. I need this job."

If someone denies violating company policy, documentation will save the day. Clearly written rules, signed statements, CCTV footage, and following the correct procedures will protect you against litigation. As one Captain said to me, "Everybody has a lawyer these days. We must do everything by the book." There are cruise industry lawyers right at the pier where cruise ships dock who are actively soliciting. They wait for the crew to debark, and will ask, "Oh, you got fired today? If you want to sue, here's my card, I'm a lawyer." They're like ambulance chasers right on the pier. Certain lawyers are well-known in the cruise industry because they make their living representing disgruntled crew and passengers.

Removing someone from their position is about more than just stopping unacceptable behavior or punishing poor performance. Our actions, and in some cases, inactions, impact others. If a server isn't fulfilling their function, their coworkers have to pick up the slack. Firing the transgressor shows everyone that they must take the rules seriously, and ultimately, rules protect everyone and maintain harmony in the work environment.

A dancer once misbehaved so badly in front of guests that he was confined to his cabin for the rest of the cruise. He was taken out of the production shows, which required re-blocking the choreography. Think about how many people were affected. An entire cast of singers and dancers, as well as all the technicians and musicians who had to attend the extra rehearsals. He was not a popular person, and was let go soon after.

IT'S BUSINESS, NOT PERSONAL

If you are faced with having to fire someone, try to remember, you are not ruining the rest of their life, despite what they might claim in the heat of the moment. In fact, many people report being relieved. They didn't really like their job anyway or felt overwhelmed or unqualified for the position but were reluctant to quit.

Not everyone who is disciplined is fired. In fact, it can help turn someone's career around. I once worked with a cruise staff member who was nearly on his way down the gangway with two written warnings. He was very good at his job, but was a free spirit and wanted to do things his way, not the correct way as determined by the cruise line. We had a heart-to-heart conversation and he finally realized he loved the cruise industry and all that it had to offer, and he turned his behavior around, became a model staff member, and is now an Assistant Cruise Director hoping to move up the ladder. He even won Employee of the Month!

SHIP TO SHORE

The lessons from these stories can easily be applied in a land-based or virtual business. Here's how:

- Create your process so that firing does not come as a surprise to the employee. It will be clear to them that it is the final step of the process.
- When you give final notice, make it clear that it is a non-negotiable decision. All debate has ended.
- Have another member of the management team in attendance for any disciplinary hearings as well as the dismissal.
- Don't discuss the details with other staff. "Yes, they were let go for a violation of policy," is the only statement you need to make.

- Do not send out a company email stating, "He is no longer with us." One of my friends received such an email and the staff thought the person had died. (You can't make this ship up, can you?)
- If possible, put the entire process into a choreographed musical number. This will offer other people in the office an opportunity to show off their natural talents. Perhaps a full office talent show? Just make it a whole thing . . . or not.

CHAPTER 10:

COME HELL OR HIGH WATER: OVERCOMING OBSTACLES

"COME HELL OR HIGH WATER" is the strongest declaration of determination in the American lexicon. As with most idioms, its origin remains moderately dubious. Dating back to early 1900s cattle ranching, the phrase is thought to refer to the hardships of cattle driving. Often traveling thousands of miles though "hell," cattle were herded across numerous rivers, hence "deep water." Cowboys had to get their herd to market come hell or high water.

Although we've never had a herd of cattle on board, we certainly know how to deal with high water. In the cruise business, another term for high water is rough seas, usually caused by rough weather. I've had the pleasure (not sure that's the right word) of going through some pretty rough weather and high seas. While no one enjoys rough weather, we always have to prepare for it, especially when it comes to the entertainment on stage.

Please let me interject something before we go any further and I get hammered by the cruise industry. Ninety-five percent of the time there are calm seas, sunny weather, and smooth sailing throughout the entire cruise. So, if you've never cruised and are nervous about rough seas, don't be. I'm talking about the other five percent of the time, which would never happen to you. Bad weather only happens on other people's cruises.

Getting back to rough weather, we do get advance notice from the bridge about weather conditions. If there are strong winds expected, we secure the heavy equipment, such as speakers and sets backstage. These days, most pianos are actually bolted to the floor, but in the old days we had to tie them up and secure them to a bulkhead. I've been through a force ten storm that flipped a piano completely over, with its legs sticking straight up in the air. One bad wave and everything goes flying: furniture, instruments, chairs, tables, glasses, you name it. We quite literally have to batten down the hatches.

One night on an Alaska cruise, we were docking during rough weather, when the bridge lost all power, which included the steering. I was in the dining room, and we just kept listing and listing and listing to one side. All the plates and glasses were falling, and the waiters were scrambling to hold everything back. Thank goodness we were going very slowly and narrowly missed crashing into the dock just as the power was restored. The Captain handled it masterfully with no injuries or accidents. Ship happens.

Now I should mention a few things. First, the movement of a ship is always the most pronounced in the front and the back of the ship (forward and aft in nautical terms), as that is where most of the movement is happening. Second, on many ships, the theater is located either in the front or the back of the ship. I'm sure the ship architects had very good reasons for designing it this way, or they just don't like show biz people. Whatever the reason, the entertainers really thank you (said dripping with sarcasm) for making their jobs just a little more difficult. Third, the show must go on. We don't cancel shows when the water gets choppy.

When the seas start to feel a bit rough, we call the bridge hours in advance of a show to see how much the ship is listing or pitching. Listing is the motion from side-to-side. Pitching is the front-to-back motion. If the ship is consistently moving more than two or three degrees each way, then we go into what's called Plan B for the production show, which means the girls take off their high heels and do the show in flat shoes. The male dancers don't lift their partners as high because the shows are very physically demanding and the stage floor may move in the middle of a lift. Patrick Swayze and Jennifer Gray never had these problems.

If there are aerialists in the show coming down from the ceiling, strapped in harnesses, we'll cut these during rough weather. The production shows on these new ships rival anything on Broadway or in Las Vegas, and are technically very complex, even in smooth seas, let alone rough weather. One of the shows has a simulated airplane (with passenger!) that flies over the audience. Another show features forty-eight drones flying above the crowd. Technology is crazy and technology is wonderful until it isn't working, especially in rough seas. Fortunately, we have very talented technicians on board who can fix it all. The only thing we have no control over is the weather.

ROUGH WEATHER DOES NOT DISCRIMINATE

It's not only production shows that are affected by rough weather. Headliners are not spared either. Back in the 1980s and 1990s, cruise lines such as Norwegian Cruise Line and Royal Caribbean had a celebrity entertainer program, spearheaded by Peter Compton, who booked some pretty big names in those days. Jerry Lewis, The Fifth Dimension, Phyllis Diller, Norm Crosby, David Brenner, The Captain & Tennille and Mary Wilson of the Supremes amongst many others, who were major stars in the 1970s, 1980s and 1990s. The guests were delighted by the surprise appearance of these celebrities because we never announced them in advance. Although it would certainly have increased sales, they couldn't promote celebrities in advance because of the possibility they might have to cancel at the last minute due to schedule conflicts, transportation issues, or weather delays.

Jim Stafford is a wonderful singer and comedian who has had a few top forty hits. You might remember one called "Spiders and Snakes." He had his own TV show in the 1970s, appeared in a few movies, and had opened a very successful theater in Branson, Missouri. Jim came on board to do a few shows for us as part of our celebrity program. He had a great show, and our guests always received him well.

We always scheduled our celebrity performers to perform on "formal" nights, and people used to get really dressed up. The men would wear suits or tuxedos and the women would wear evening gowns. We had two shows: the early seating diners would attend the 8:30 p.m. show, and the late seating diners would attend the 10:30 p.m. show after their meal.

It was night six of a seven-day cruise. A few hours from port, we hit some rough weather out in the Caribbean. During Jim's first show, the seas continued to surge, and the waves got worse—probably hitting ten to fifteen feet.

Jim was on stage about halfway through the show, telling jokes, singing, playing guitar, backed up by a twelve-piece orchestra. The audience was having a wonderful time. Everything was going great, except of course, the weather, which was getting worse. The ship was not only listing from side to side, it was also pitching back and forth. The next thing I know, Jim strode off stage in the middle of a song and the orchestra kept playing. A few minutes later, Jim calmly walked back onto the stage, picked up his guitar, and continued to play.

Turns out, this was Jim's first cruise in rough weather, and he had no idea that he was subject to sea sickness. Now, I've never been seasick (thank you Lord), but people say it is a terrible experience; in addition to feeling nauseous, it makes you very, very weak. It can last two hours or two days, or at least until the ship gets closer to land and the waves lessen.

Pro that he is, Jim ran off stage just long enough to locate a trash can, dive headfirst into it, and get sick. He then proceeded to stand up, brush himself off, return to the stage and finish the show—albeit a bit green around the gills. The audience did not have any idea what Jim was going through.

As Jim finished his performance, he got even sicker. He walked off stage on wobbly legs and by the time I got backstage to check on him, he was flat on his back. There was no question; he was unable to go on with the second show. While his manager helped Jim back to his cabin, I had to come up with a plan. There were about thirty minutes before the second show started and people were coming into the house, finding their seats. With Jim unable to perform, this meant that half the passengers wouldn't get to see the celebrity performance.

We had thirty minutes to come up with a plan. What were we going to do? We decided after some back and forth conversation with the Production Manager, Musical Director and Jim's manager that we would arrange for the second seating crowd who missed tonight's performance to see a matinee performance at 5:00 p.m. the next day. They would then get to see the regularly scheduled Farewell Show later that night. I checked with everyone else involved in the operation (Bar Manager to make sure there was bar staff available, the ACD to make sure final Bingo would be finished in time) and then informed the Hotel Director of the situation. He was very happy we had it all under control.

I walked onstage as if starting a show but had to give them the bad news: "I am so sorry, but we have a bit of a situation right now. We don't have a show for you tonight." I explained that Jim was flat on his back and there no way would he could perform. But I did have good news for them. I explained how they would get to see the show the next afternoon, as well as all the other great activities and events we had planned. They would not miss anything. Naturally, many people were disappointed. Some, however, became incensed (there are always a few). But the majority were very understanding, especially since we were able to let them know we had already come up with a plan for them to see the show the next day. They were appreciative that we worked fast to find a solution. And of course, they could feel the strong ship motion and bad weather and felt bad for Jim. The big band played a few numbers as people began to leave.

The next morning dawned sunny; the seas were much calmer,

and Mother Nature, God bless her, can make for the roughest seas one day, and the next day it's smooth as glass. Jim's stomach had also settled. He was only too happy to perform at 5:00 p.m. The theater was standing room only and he did a fantastic show, even making fun of himself and his dilemma the night before.

It actually worked out really well. We came up with the schedule and let folks know what was happening, all on the fly. Although we couldn't put the changes in our daily printed program because it had already been printed for the final day, we made announcements throughout the next day and had a packed show at five o'clock.

One thing I made sure to do was inform the Guest Services Desk about the change in Jim's show for the next day, as they are the ones who get hit with all the questions at all hours of the day and night. They needed to know the change in plans because people went to the front desk asking, "Oh, I heard the show was canceled. What are the plans for tomorrow?" The first thing that happens when there's confusion is everybody goes to, or calls, the front desk, which is open twenty-four hours a day. We needed to keep them informed about what was happening, so they were not caught unprepared. It takes the entire team to implement changes. The same is true with any land-based businesses. When changes are made to your product or service, your front-line employees, those who deal with the public every day, need to be the first to know so they don't come across as ill prepared or unknowledgeable.

The lesson for us all is to always have a backup plan. Your business may not face rough seas and force ten storms, but there will be things like missed deliveries, weather closings, flooding, power outages, computer failures, and security breaches. Be prepared for the disasters that may come your way, and stay flexible. When you know well in advance how to respond, you will be prepared to lead and will not succumb to panic. As the saying goes, "Fail to prepare, prepare to fail." When you project calm, you will get your team on board and instill confidence in their abilities.

Sometimes, having a Plan B isn't enough. If the seas are consistently bad, there is a Plan C. Weather might be so bad they have to cancel all the other performers and bring on a comedian who doesn't require any props or sets. He can sit motionless on the stage strapped to a chair and tell jokes. (Just kidding, we love our comedians. It is not easy to do what they do...and they really don't like being strapped to chairs.) If the seas are really bad, pretty much everybody will be in their cabin, sick anyway, and we show a movie in the theater for the hardy ones who have ventured out.

It takes a lot of people to design and execute contingency plans and communication is key. Everybody needs to be rowing in the same direction. Changing a performance impacts more than just one performer.

When the ratings came in after the Jim Stafford cruise, everybody was very happy. We had come up with a workable solution that met everyone's needs. Jim had time to recover and the passengers received the full entertainment package they expected.

FOG DID WHAT?

There are times when the weather is so bad, or the fog is too thick that the ships can't go into port. There have been ships that are supposed to end a cruise, and five days later, they're still sitting in the harbor because the port is closed. Galveston, Texas is a big port (everything is bigger in Texas) where fog comes in frequently, and the cruise has ended and people who were supposed to get off on a Sunday and go home are still on board the ship the next Friday because the port's been closed by the government authorities due to the adverse weather.

And it's not just in the Caribbean. I was sailing on a ship out of Baltimore, Maryland in the winter when a very bad snowstorm closed the port and the ship could not dock until the next day. The passengers on board got a free day, but the people waiting in

Baltimore for the next cruise were shorted a day. Some guests were happy, some weren't.

THE PHONE CALL YOU NEVER WANT TO GET

If there's a really bad storm, we sometimes have to miss a port of call. An emergency day at sea. Oh, what a joy. I love getting that phone call at five or six in the morning telling me, "Sorry, Paul, we're missing port today, bad weather, get your team ready for an emergency sea day." If you really want an entire ship mad at you, both guests and crew, tell them they're missing a port of call and must stay on the ship all day. I can feel the love now.

Plus I'm thinking, *Holy crap, there's an entertainer waiting to join us today in Grand Cayman who is supposed to perform tomorrow night. I don't have an extra act on board.* Every act is scheduled on a certain night. By missing a port of call when an entertainer is waiting to join the ship, we need to get that entertainer to the next port, or come up with a whole new show. Thank you, rough weather.

WEDDING BELL BLUES

Who doesn't love a beautiful wedding? The planning, the anticipation, the dress, the food, the terrible speeches, the music, the family and friends; it's just an exciting time of a couple's life. Weddings are big business in the cruise industry. Planning a wedding on board a cruise ship can be an easy, stress-free process for all involved. (Ha, who am I kidding, stress-free? Yea, right, it is a wedding after all.) Everything is in one place. You have the venue, professional photographers and videographers, wonderful food options, a DJ or live band, and an on board wedding planner right there for you.

Now I should mention there are two basic types of weddings that can occur. The first is an onboard wedding as described above, which usually happens on embarkation day while in port. After the wedding is over, most guests leave the ship, and the happy couple remains on board for their honeymoon (hopefully with a happier ending than the honeymoon in Chapter 1).

The other type of wedding is called a destination wedding, where the happy couple wants to get married on one of the Caribbean islands that we visit, usually on the beach. This is arranged through the cruise line shore side wedding coordinator, with all the paperwork handled in advance with the government where the wedding is taking place. Unfortunately, all the islands are not under one government, so the official wedding documents are only good for that one island.

And for the most part, the majority of weddings planned with cruise lines are perfect and go off without a hitch. For the most part.

Occasionally, rarely, a few times, sometimes, things might not go according to plan. Sometimes it's the fault of the cruise line, sometimes it's not. When they are the fault of the cruise line, they are usually quick fixes that are handled immediately right on site by a very professional team. When it is not the fault of the cruise line, well then it gets a bit tricky.

Here are two similar stories that unfortunately have two different endings.

Destination Wedding No. 1: David and Nancy booked their destination wedding on the beautiful island of Grand Cayman, with its white sandy beaches, cool breeze and beautiful weather. We were on a seven-day cruise from Miami, Florida, and Grand Cayman was the fourth day of the cruise. There was a group of family members from both sides of the wedding party sailing on board, and some friends had actually flown to the island to be there with David and Nancy when they arrived to tie the knot. It was going to be wonderful.

Destination Wedding No. 2: Rod and Debra planned their wedding on the gorgeous pink sand beaches of Bermuda. Their five-day cruise was sailing out of Baltimore, Maryland, and was scheduled to be in Bermuda for two and a half days, as it was the only port on the itinerary. Around 200 of Rod and Debra's friends and family were sailing on the cruise to celebrate their nuptials. They had flown in from all over the world, as Rod and Debra worked in the international sector. It was going to be wonderful.

Both cruises were years apart, but they had one similarity.

They were both booked DURING HURRICANE SEASON!

You know, that time every year from June 1 to December 1 when those pesky hurricanes can form and wreak havoc across wide swatches of the Caribbean and Atlantic. They say rain on your wedding day is lucky. Hurricanes are a whole different story.

Would you like to render a guess as to what happened during these two cruises? Bingo—you won! Massive hurricanes formed and headed towards those islands. Of course, the wedding couples were monitoring the weather forecast leading up to the cruises, but there was very little they could do except to pray the weather gods would be on their side. Which they weren't.

You should know cruise ships will avoid hurricanes at all costs. The No. 1 responsibility of the Captain is the safety and well-being of the passengers, crew, and the ship. So, if a hurricane looks like it is heading towards a particular region (western Caribbean, eastern Caribbean, etc.) they will run and hide and go find sunny weather and calm seas in a different region. Passengers may be disappointed they did not get to go to the originally scheduled ports of call, but they are extremely happy they went to warm, sunny destinations with calm seas and no hurricanes. I should tell you the ship can make it through a powerful hurricane with no problems. But it's the passengers and crew that will find it very difficult. Very rough seas are not something you want to go through for any length of time. Ask Jim Stafford, he'll tell you. The Captain will not put anyone in harm's way.

So, in both situations, we did not make it to the ports of call for the couples to get married. Of course, they were both disappointed. But while David and Nancy were able to visit nice destinations with great weather (St. Thomas, St. Maarten), their friends who flew to Grand Cayman to join them for their wedding were now stuck on the island bracing for the hurricane, as the airports were shut down and no flights were leaving. Talk about a double whammy.

With Rod and Debra, it really was a double whammy, as two hurricanes approached Bermuda, one from the west and one from the south. So that really hampered where the ship could go, especially since it was only a five-day cruise. We couldn't travel south because we would hit that hurricane, and going north had few potential ports within a five-day span. So, we ended up sailing from Baltimore to New York, where we spent three days before heading back to Baltimore. And wouldn't you know it, Rod and Debra were from New York! So, they flew from New York to Baltimore for a cruise that took them right back to New York. Can you say "unhappy campers?" And more importantly, "unhappy bride?"

But they booked their destination wedding DURING HURRICANE SEASON. What could we do?

Actually, we did a lot. In both instances, we pampered the wedding couples each and every day. We sent them to the spa for couples' massages, we sent them to the specialty dining restaurants for romantic meals, we sent champagne and chocolate covered strawberries to their staterooms. We tried to make them as comfortable as possible. We wanted them to feel special despite the circumstances. We empathized.

In the case of David and Nancy, our onboard staff worked incredibly hard with our shore side team to organize the paperwork and documentation so they could get married on board the ship the morning we arrived back in Miami at the end of the seven-day cruise. We arranged for a justice of the peace to come on board, and they got married at 8:00 a.m. with their families around them, before disembarking and then heading home. So, they had the honeymoon before the wedding. Now that's an interesting concept. Have the honeymoon first. Needless to say, everyone was extremely happy with the way things turned out. Except for the friends stuck on Grand Cayman.

Rod and Debra had a different ending. They were going to wait to get back home before deciding anything definite. There was not enough time for them to get married in Baltimore. Remember, they had hundreds of people fly in from all over the world for this wedding, so they didn't want to plan another big wedding again. They really appreciated what we did for them, but knew we couldn't control the weather.

They did have one special request. They wanted to have their first official dance together with their friends present, even though they weren't officially married. So, on the last night of the cruise, we arranged for the band to play their special song right in the nine-deck atrium, the center of the ship, where all of their friends, as well as much of the ship could watch and cheer them on. The bride wore her beautiful wedding gown and the groom his very sharp tuxedo. I made a special announcement to introduce them, and the crowd went wild, especially since they knew that their wedding was cancelled due to the hurricane. Needless to say, a few tears were shed.

We wished them the best, but know their expectations of leaving the ship married were not met.

My lesson for the day: Don't book a destination wedding in the Caribbean DURING HURRICANE SEASON!

You're welcome.

SHIP TO SHORE

You may not have to prepare for disasters of *Titanic* proportions, but you definitely want to have a Plan B. Here are some tips to consider:

- Do some brainstorming. What kind of emergencies are you likely to face in your business? Weather impacts land-based businesses—wind, storms, snow, and ice can cause transportation problems and closings.

- The internet has a huge impact on business when it goes down. It can be weather-related or provider issues. Being able to communicate effectively is key, so consider this when making Plan A, B, and C.

- Dozens of people are involved with decision-making and implementing, so part of your contingency plans has to include the "who" in addition to the "what" and the "when." Ask yourself "**When** this happens, **who** will be doing **what**?"

- Don't wait for a crisis or emergency to start thinking about contingency plans. By then it is too late. Plan in advance so you can turn right to it, and everyone will be on the same page.

- Brides, if you think a can of Aqua Net hair spray can withstand a hurricane, you're wrong. You'll need two cans.

Jim Stafford on a better day with calm seas.

CHAPTER 11:

WE'RE ALL IN THE SAME BOAT: LEADING WITH EMPATHY

MOST OF OUR PROBLEMS can be solved if we just talk about them (wow, what a concept!) But there needs to be someone who is compassionate enough to listen with an empathetic ear. We talk a lot about rules and procedures and policies for running a tight ship; equally important is empathy. It is one of those EQ qualities that makes a good leader. Your company may have great products and great service, and yet, your business is nothing without great people. The best leaders are trusted, not feared. Can your people trust you with their problems?

Empathy is "the ability to understand and share the feelings of another person." Nothing is more powerful in a customer service interaction than an employee who genuinely empathizes with a customer and his or her situation. And while some people believe you are born with this quality, empathy is something that can actually be learned. We can all take the time to imagine ourselves in someone else's shoes and allow ourselves to imagine what that person is going through. Trying to understand what another person is feeling starts with a willingness to listen. And while not every employee can solve every problem, they can always show empathy.

To be your most empathetic self, remember:

- Be present and in the moment; put away distractions. No one can solve a problem when they are on their phones checking social media. You come across as disinterested when you're not giving your full attention.

- Listen without interrupting. It usually takes only two minutes for customers to explain their concerns.
- Don't be judgmental. You are only aware of a fraction of the circumstances that created this situation. Compassion goes a long way.
- Be respectful. Even if you don't agree with what the customer is saying, or how they are saying it, stay polite and calm. The customer may not always be right, but they are always the customer, and they always think they're right.
- If you are dealing with someone in person, look for non-verbal communication signs such as facial expressions and tone of voice. You can learn a lot from what they don't say.
- Make sure you understand the problem or situation thoroughly before taking action. Repeat back what you understand as the issue to ensure everyone is on the same page.
- Include a module on empathy as part of your corporate training program for all employees, not just those on the front lines.

Empathy is triggered on an emotional level when we understand how another person feels, and that comes from finding common ground. We all want to be happy. We all want to be heard. We all feel pain and suffer loss. Whenever you have the chance to hear someone else's story, listen with the goal of giving them a chance to share the events that have shaped their lives. Appreciate the opportunity to gain understanding of a path that can be significantly different than your own.

We are not all born with empathy, but again, I firmly believe we can all learn it. I have definitely developed a better understanding of the human condition since my Boston University days. Traveling around the world is the best education anyone could have. It allows you to see other people's realities. Life is very different just 100 miles away from home. Working and living with people of all ages, from over a hundred countries, has increased my understanding of other cultures, traditions, and values.

I've been to Haiti with its beautiful waterfalls and vibrant arts community— contrasted with a high crime rate and crushing poverty. Some of the buildings in Yemen date back thousands of years and remain standing despite a history of frequent civil war. I've seen the chasm between the very rich and the very poor on the same street in Venezuela. I've witnessed the effects of communism in various countries around the world, and the results of an atomic bomb blast in Japan. I witness all these things, then step back on board where I'm greeted by luxury and safety, and sometimes I feel guilty for it. I realize how fortunate and blessed I am. One moment of gratitude can change your perspective on just about anything.

Kindness goes a long way toward understanding. Over the years, many crew members have suffered personal losses while away from home. Some cruise lines offer a two-week compassionate leave to go home for a funeral or family emergency and their job will be there for them when they get back. But on some lines they must pay their own way home. Some of these people live halfway around the world and a roundtrip ticket can cost thousands of dollars. Furthermore, many crew send home nearly all of their pay to help support family members and have very little cash aboard. These crew members are our family, and we've seen many of them suffer tragedies. When tragedy strikes one of our own, it's amazing to watch the crew come together and create a collection fund to pay for the ticket home or emergency expenses.

Furthermore, the company does not send out a replacement for two weeks, so other crew members must cover the absence of someone on compassionate leave. People will pick up more duties, or sometimes activities are rearranged, and everyone pitches in to cover for each other.

EVERYONE HAS A STORY YOU KNOW NOTHING ABOUT

As a manager, it is up to you to create an environment that feels safe for others to share their challenges. When people are afraid to share events in their personal life, it can lead to greater misunderstandings. They may fear their personal circumstances make them appear weak. They may fear the judgement of their coworkers. Maybe they have money troubles or they lost custody of their child.

Equally, some staff are afraid to share work challenges for fear of reprisal, or fear of creating the impression they can't handle the job.

The common thread is that people are afraid of not knowing what is going to happen, so their imagination takes them to the worst possible scenario. They become fearful, and most of the time, the terrible thing they think is going to happen never does. You may know the acronym, F.E.A.R. which stands for "False Evidence Appearing Real." More often than not the outcome is never as bad as we imagined. We always play mind games with ourselves on what the worst possible conclusion is going to be in any situation.

We've probably all worked places where somebody goes silent, or they don't come in for a few days and you have no idea what's going on. Are they hung over or are they dealing with a very serious issue?

No matter what the situation, we do not want to force people to share personal details, but rather, create an environment where they feel safe doing so.

Anything and everything that happens on land happens on a ship. If you have loneliness and depression on land, you certainly have loneliness and depression on a ship. If there is harassment on land, you have harassment on a ship. The ship really is a microcosm of everything that happens in society. A great leader leads with empathy and strives to create an environment where employees feel safe to engage in difficult conversations.

MAKE THE SPACE TO LISTEN

As a Cruise Director, I socialize with guests, often before shows. When I walk through the theater, I hear some inspiring stories from people who have faced incredible odds, from illnesses and bankruptcies to rekindled romances and finding long-lost family members. I've heard, "Our last vacation was over twenty years ago," or, "This is my first cruise since my husband passed away." Some stories really pull at your heart strings. One couple told me, "It's our fiftieth anniversary. We've been putting away a little bit every month to save up for this trip." It makes me so happy that I get to be a part of their experience and help them create more wonderful memories.

Countless times people have said to me, "This vacation has been so good, it's so needed, it's our trip of a lifetime." It is important to listen, whether you are the Captain of the ship or the guy pouring coffee. You meet someone who is a complete jerk and the last thing you want to do is listen to them talk. But you don't know, maybe they're just a jerk, or maybe they are barely holding onto civility because they've just lost their business or their mother.

Whether you are listening to your customer, your client, your co-worker, or your boss, one of the most important steps to being a good listener is to stop what you are doing and pay attention. Compassionate listening skills aren't taught in school, or as part of an MBA. It is something anyone can learn.

And the stories I hear: Somebody from the Philippines is trying to put four kids through college on their assistant waiter salary and their house just got washed away in a tsunami. A waiter from Jamaica is working full time on board with a small child at home while still completing college courses online in her spare time. So inspiring.

Even when I get a call from a solicitor at home, I listen. They're just trying to make a sale. I listen and say, "Thank you so much. I appreciate you thinking about me, but I'm just not interested." (Okay, sometimes I'm not that nice, but I can have a bad day too.) There is no reason you can't treat people with respect. You don't have to swear at them and hang up in their face. They are probably getting chewed out on nearly every other phone call. That has got to wear on even the thickest-skinned people.

Being able to put yourself in somebody else's situation is so important and so key. I really want to stress how important empathy is. You can't put everything in a manual. You can't tell someone to feel compassionate. When Jane comes to you with her personal problems, you need to act with compassion, and by the simple act of putting yourself in the other person's shoes (empathy), you are indeed building that compassion muscle.

TRAGEDY BRINGS US TOGETHER

"Paul, have you seen the news?"

"No, what's going on?" I inquired, never expecting what I was about to witness.

"Just turn on the TV."

Most of you are old enough to remember where you were when you heard about the World Trade Center attack on September 11, 2001. I happened to be on board *Enchantment of the Seas* sailing into Cozumel, Mexico for the day.

I had a small TV in my office, so I flipped it on. Suffice it to say, I was glued to the TV for what seemed like forever. I saw the first tower go down around 9:00 a.m. Cozumel time, and the second tower not much later, and knew life would never be the same.

Many guests were already off the ship, wanting to get an early start on their day, but many guests were still on board, and the news started to spread quickly. The mood changed dramatically from happy, festive vacationers to concerned world citizens. By the time everyone got back on board by 5:00 p.m., the world was a completely different place.

My phone started ringing off the hook that morning. Emergency meeting with the senior officers in the Captain's office in fifteen minutes. The first of many, many meetings that day and for weeks to follow. We had a conference call with all the ships in our fleet around the world and our shore side executive management team. We were constantly getting updates. All planes flying into the U.S. were grounded. Airports closed. We were not sure that first day which ports would be open to welcome back cruise ships. How would we get all of our guests home if there were no planes flying, and how would guests scheduled to join us for the next cruise get to Miami? So many questions and very few answers. The one thing we did know was that the world would never be the same.

I was immediately faced with how to schedule the rest of the day, as well as the rest of the cruise, which still had five days remaining. Nobody, and I mean nobody, on board was in any sort of mood to have fun and party. Should we have shows that night? What about activities? What should the Captain say over the PA system when everyone returned to the ship? Some Captains were better at this than others.

As the day wore on, we started to get answers. We would run the cruise as scheduled with regard to activities and entertainment. Our corporate communications department sent all the Captains a short message to read over the PA system, so that everyone was on the same page. We let our guests know that as soon as we had updated information, we would relate it to them immediately. We kept them informed.

As far as my division was concerned, it was up to us to convey some sort of normalcy. All activities ran as scheduled. We were lucky that the scheduled entertainment for that evening was a production show starring our singers and dancers. This was not a night for comedy, and I learned some other ships had comedians scheduled to perform but had to quickly pivot to other shows at the last minute. I am sure the comedians that were scheduled to work that night were relieved they didn't have to perform.

I met with the cast during the afternoon, and they all said they were happy to perform that night, and felt it was good for our passengers. I was grateful for their great attitude and willingness to help out. But I had to go out and introduce the entertainment that night. At no time in my years of training did I ever have a class on what to say to a group of people on the day an international tragedy rocks the world. I was extremely fortunate that a wonderful entertainer, comedy magician Bruce Gold was sailing with us that cruise. He was scheduled to perform later in the week. He is a gifted writer and good friend, and he met me backstage about fifteen minutes before the show was about to start. He asked me if I knew what I was going to say, as he knew the gravity of the situation. I told him I was thinking about a few things and asked for his suggestions. He quickly rattled off two or three very comforting things to say which perfectly fit the moment. I was eternally grateful, as his thoughts coincided with what I wanted to say.

Usually when the show starts, the band plays my intro music ("Soul Vaccination" by Tower of Power if you really want to know), but I didn't think a musical intro would be fitting for the occasion. After the lights went down, I calmly walked out on stage and welcomed everyone to the theater. It was obviously a somber mood.

I welcomed them to the show and of course mentioned the tragedy. I then said: "For those of you who are with loved ones right now, make sure to give them an extra hug tonight, and tell them how much you love them. As we found out today, nothing in life is guaranteed."

I went on to say that we wanted to bring them entertainment that evening, not so we could sweep what happened under the rug, but to take their minds off what happened for just an hour. "I met with the cast earlier in the day, and they were very sincere in their wish to perform tonight." The audience then gave them a big round of applause before the show even started.

I closed the introduction with, "We are holding a memorial service later in the cruise on a sea day. If anyone wants to get involved, please see me after the show." That turned out to be one of the best things we did, to bring everyone together so we could grieve as a group. There was clergy on board who volunteered to help (it was a non-religious service) as well as some guests who were from New York and had family at the World Trade Center that day but made it safely home. They all spoke at the service and brought a perspective and humanity that we greatly needed.

The service was held at 11:00 a.m. the next sea day, and the theater was standing room only, so we decided to broadcast the service to the staterooms for the rest of that day. People from all different countries, religions, and walks of life attended. We had music from some of the musicians on board, responsive readings, as well as moments of reflection. It lasted about an hour and suffice it to say, it was quite emotional. It seemed that as soon as we finished the service, a black cloud lifted. While the purpose was not to forget or dismiss what had happened a few days earlier, the service gave everyone permission to breathe and take stock of what had happened and how their lives were affected. We received many positive comments about how we handled the situation, and it was one of the highest rated cruises of the year.

But the travel industry was forever changed. The next week the ship was less than half-full, as many people started getting cold feet about flying so soon. We offered our guests who were on board during the tragedy the opportunity to stay with us for the next cruise—we were basically giving the cabins away. We had a few takers who were in no rush to get home. The ships remained fairly empty for the next few months, until we slowly returned to some sort of normalcy. Eventually our guests started to return in full force, but safety and security procedures had changed forever: Metal detectors installed on all gangways, pictures embedded on all passenger and crew cards, and increased safety and security training for the crew, among other safety and security measures.

Never forget.

SHIP TO SHORE

No matter what business you are in, here are some tips that will help you lead with empathy:

- Leadership comes from any position within the company.
- Empathy is one of the most important "soft skills."
- Open yourself up to listening to others' experiences.
- Hire from a diverse pool of qualified people.
- Create opportunities for people to share their story.
- Take steps toward understanding motivations.
- Listen without judging or offering an instant solution.

CHAPTER 12:

BABY ON BOARD

"YOU'VE COME A LONG WAY, BABY."

That has to be one of the most memorable advertising slogans of all time. In 1968, Phillip Morris hired the Leo Burnett Agency to develop a campaign for Virginia Slims cigarettes to exploit the women's liberation movement. One such ad used headline copy that read, "We make Virginia Slims for women because they are biologically superior to men," and featured a woman wearing a superhero costume. Other ads showed women wearing pants and women of color. Women may have come a long way as targets in advertising, but the working world was a different story. In 1968, women were earning on average only fifty-eight percent of what their male counterparts were. We've made a lot of progress since then, recognizing the addictive and deadly dangers of smoking, but how much progress have we made with gender pay equity?

By the 80s, after I started in the cruise industry, the gender wage gap had narrowed only slightly to sixty-one to sixty-six percent. On board, women in general were either performers, cruise and youth staff, shore excursion staff, or pursers and definitely a minority in a very old school, male majority mindset with many stereotypes. In those days, there were very few female room stewards or stateroom attendants and no females in the dining rooms; it was all men. The first time a woman went in as a supervisor in the dining room, the backlash was incredible. The male crew, many of whom were from countries less progressive than the United States when it came to women's equality, weren't having it. They didn't want to have anything to do with a woman being in charge.

Kara Boyd became my assistant in 1997 and is seriously a go-getter—full of energy, enthusiasm, and creative ideas. She comes from a family of six girls and one boy. Over the years, we became very good friends and I have taken a great deal of pleasure watching her groundbreaking career success. Kara moved on to another cruise line and became a four-stripe Cruise Director. Four stripe officers report directly to the Captain instead of the Hotel Director and are part of the Shipboard Executive Steering Committee, consisting of the Captain, Staff Captain, Chief Engineer, Hotel Director, Human Resource Manager, Finance Manager, and Cruise Director. It was a very high honor for Kara.

As if achieving Cruise Director status in a male dominated field wasn't enough, Kara's career trajectory became the catalyst for rewriting infant and family policy at her cruise line, one of the world's largest family entertainment and media companies, so a lot was at stake. Kara's daughter, Alanna, spent the first three years of her life at sea with her parents while her mom continued to lead the entertainment department, delivering the highest quality guest experience.

Kara has shared with me: "Looking back on it now, I didn't realize how groundbreaking it was, but they are a very inclusive company; they've always been out in front." They began writing and rewriting child and infant policies based on Kara's experience for female officers who are also working parents at sea. It begs the question: How many land-based businesses allow their employees to bring their children to work every day?

KARA'S JOURNEY

Kara and I recently caught up via video chat and I'll let her tell you about her career at sea in her own words. Here's what she has to say:

This is one of my favorite subjects because it is near and dear to my heart. It's one of my proudest achievements, but it was never, ever easy.

I was already a Cruise Director for another cruise line before they hired me. At the time, they were building three new ships and they promised if I came on as Assistant Cruise Director (ACD) for just one contract, then I would move up to Cruise Director as soon as one of the new ships was finished. I didn't want to take a step down, but I had a love for this company and thought this was the right move for me. Besides, my husband, Tim, was a bandleader on the ship and it meant we could be together. I took the ACD job and three months later, 9/11 happened. The cruise industry was in turmoil and they decided that it was not the right time to build three new ships. This meant that I was not going to get my promotion to Cruise Director. I decided to wait it out, and in the meantime, Tim and I decided to start a family. This was 2001, and everyone was talking about being a family company and being accepting and tolerant of a female in the workplace, but there still was a stigma, and I was actually afraid to speak openly about how I wanted a family, because I didn't want that to hurt my promotion possibilities.

I was already 37—that biological clock was ticking, and I was a little nervous about that. I thought, well, you know what, I have to do what's best for us and God will provide. Hopefully the company will say that I can still perform, even if I have a baby. I started talking to HR and looking at the maternity policy. I was really blessed to have a wonderful senior female leader, Kathy, in HR shore side, to walk me through the journey. This was critical because I couldn't have these conversations openly, because nobody had ever done this before, and even if they supported it in their hearts, they had their operational concerns.

And as life happens, everything happened at once! I was promoted to "Step Up" Cruise Director, which meant I would do a three-month contract with a month as Assistant Cruise Director and then take over as Cruise Director for two months while the Senior Cruise Director was on vacation. It was what I had been waiting for and then during that year, I also found out we were expecting!

I still remember the day that I found out I was pregnant. Tim was already up on stage leading the Sail Away show, doing his rock and roll thing, so I couldn't share the news with him. It was in the middle of my workday as well and I went on stage to do my show. As cruise ship life happens, you have your welcome aboard show, then you have a meeting, and Tim was doing sets until midnight. I started work early in the day and he works til late at night. He was always starving when he got in, so I ordered him a tuna fish sandwich from Room Service and left him a little note that read, "Dear Daddy, I hope you enjoy your tuna fish sandwich. Can't wait to meet. Love, Your Baby." Then I went to bed. Needless to say, I'm excited and only sleeping lightly when I hear him come in. I can tell he has read the note, but he's not saying a thing or even reacting. I had to get up and explain it to him, "Honey, we're having a baby." We had definitely made some pixie dust magic!

I wanted to keep my pregnancy low key, but I did confide in another female Cruise Director who guided me to talk to HR. We had a wonderful female HR Vice President and another female HR Director, and together we sat down and reviewed the current child policy. Would the same have happened if any of them were male? I don't think I would have received the same support.

I would be able to continue working after the baby was born, but my role had the responsibility of an emergency station so I would need to have a nanny on board because in an emergency situation, those duties would take priority and there would need to be someone else to take charge of the baby. Even though we had an onboard nursery, that was for our paying guests, and the officer's children were only accommodated based upon availability during nursery hours.

I was nervous about perception and I was nervous, to be honest, to tell some of my male leaders on board such as the Captains, Hotel Directors, even Cruise Directors. I didn't want this to hurt my promotion, so I voiced that with my HR leadership team, who decided, "We would treat this like any other situation. If you have this baby on board and you are doing your job and following the policies, there would not be an issue. If there is a performance issue, we're going to talk to you about it like we would talk to any team member who is not meeting expectations, whether their children are on board or not."

I was so excited that I didn't have to give up my dream job because I really wanted to be a Cruise Director and I wanted to have a family and also have my family on board with me. I wanted it all and I had the confidence that I could be a working mom, wife, and yes, Cruise Director that still delivers exceptional service and experiences.

As a senior officer, I was allowed to have my family in my cabin, which not many positions allow. If my husband wasn't working on board, he would have been allowed to sail with me and our baby in my cabin. Our situation was different because my husband was a musician, so he was already on board with his own cabin and was working nights. A lot of the officers had their wives on board with their children, but the wives were not working.

My first cousin, Mary Jo, and I are very close, more like sisters. She had her PhD and wanted to focus on her writing, so she said, "I'll come sail with you and take care of the baby while you're working and do my writing in my free time."

Being able to work and be pregnant and keep up with everything and keep my stamina was a challenge in itself. Once I reached twenty-two weeks they had to keep adjusting my costumes. The crew seamstress, Benita, used to say to me, "Ms. Kara, you getting a little bigger and bigger." I finally had to say to her, "Benita, I'm pregnant." And she was so happy for me! I wasn't trying to hide it, but I was trying to keep it discreet. But you know, the guests loved to hear it. And eventually people were catching on and being very sweet and supportive. But I also had a hard time knowing that there were tons of crew members who had babies at home, who were housekeepers or food servers, living in cabins that were a quarter of the size of my cabin with bunk beds, missing their babies back home. They would share their family stories and it really pulled at my heart; I felt so grateful that I would be able to keep my child with me.

As my delivery date approached, I used my vacation time as my maternity leave. Meanwhile, my husband was at sea until the week our baby was due. I was determined to wait for him to get home. Thankfully, Tim disembarked the ship on a Sunday and Alanna was born the next day! She waited for Daddy to come home. Our perfect baby girl arrived on a lovely October morning.

The company was going to give me my normal contract. The policy is after your vacation, you need to return. But after my vacation, the baby was not old enough yet and the leadership team was wonderful. They said, "The policy is you have to accept the next contract we offer you after your vacation. So, we're just not going to offer you a contract until the baby is three months old." So that was something they did to adjust the rules slightly, but it was still within their policy and they felt comfortable about it. And I was grateful because then I was able to be home for three months, although I wasn't paid. Looking back now, I see maternity policies that have evolved and now even the dads get maternity leave, and the women get paid maternity leave. It is amazing to see companies recognize child bonding is necessary for both parents.

It was time for me to start my new contract. I have my dream job and my family is going to be together. Mary Jo is lined up as nanny. We've got all the baby stuff we need and could possibly fit into the cabin. My life couldn't be more perfect. There was just one hitch; the day we are to depart, Alanna is one week shy of being three months old and management will not budge on this issue. I asked to delay one more week but was denied. This was the first challenge, and I was being tested. If I refused, the contract would be breached, and I could technically be let go. I didn't want to leave my newborn but I had to prove that I would not be intimidated and although it was challenging, as a family we decided to face it. My husband and Mary Jo stayed home with the baby that week, and I went to sea with mixed emotions and a heavy heart.

I had to go on board, be happy, do my role as Assistant Cruise Director, and be separated from my baby for the first time. It was a really tough first week. I had all the baby stuff already in the cabin, so I'm looking at the playpen and I'm looking at her crib and I'm just really emotional, but I'm putting on a really strong face because the last thing I want to be read as is an "emotional mom." I'm going above and beyond everything I can do just to be that star team player, but I'd go back to my cabin and cry every night. To be honest, I resented the lack of judgement and flexibility. But it gave me insight to future challenges and made me realize I would have to be stronger.

Mary Jo had to fly out to join us the following week instead of boarding in Port Canaveral, which was a very big sacrifice for her because she hates to fly. So, she too went above and beyond. From then on out, basically, the three of us tag-teamed the whole time. I'm very lucky because the age policy has changed and now an accompanying baby must be six months old, and for longer than seven-day cruises, the baby has to be a year old. There is sincere gratitude in hindsight.

It wasn't all smooth sailing. I have to say there were many men and an "old school" Captain who were not really on board with female officers in the first place. I did have some tough times. There were people who were constantly questioning my abilities. They were concerned about the baby's safety and my safety and my being able to do my job in an emergency situation. I understand that, but I do feel like I was targeted more than anyone else. In some ways, I always felt like I was under the microscope but in so many ways, this was an amazing success that should have been promoted and celebrated!

We had a fire one night on the ship when I was Cruise Director and at the time Mary Jo had taken another job and we had a different nanny. We called him the "Manny" because he was actually a man! Steve was the retired husband of our on board nurse. He had been in the health industry and was a grandfather and he was a gentle giant at six-foot-three. He worked out perfectly. My favorite picture of that time was Steve walking side-by-side with Alanna coming up to his knee. They had a special bond and we remain friends to this day. We had the same schedule and he already had a cabin, so I didn't have to provide a cabin for him. I could not have asked for a better caretaker. As such a big guy, he looked hysterical when he would walk Alanna while she was pushing her toy stroller.

Our arrangement was put to the test when Alanna was two and a half years old. The fire alarm went off. "Brightstar, Brightstar," the code words, were being broadcast on the ship-wide loudspeaker. Steve's wife, the ship's nurse, already had the emergency radio tuned in, and we had a plan. If we ever hear the emergency signal or even the first announcement, Steve would come to my cabin and get the baby. So as soon as I heard the first alarm, before I was fully dressed, while I was still putting my shoes on—Steve was at my door. I said, "She's sleeping. I'm going to the bridge." I left and beat almost every navigational officer or bridge team member that was supposed to be there except for the Captain, fully dressed in my stripes, ready to go on target.

We handled the situation. Thankfully, it was not a big fire and was contained in a few hours. We didn't have to go to guest evacuation or even muster stations. After that, the Captain called me in and he said, "I have some concerns, because you were on the bridge, but what if your nanny couldn't make it?"

I explained our policy to the Captain. "This is how I handle these situations. We have a detailed plan and we do practice runs. We exercise this. We practice this. We have actually timed how long it takes for him to get to my cabin in an emergency situation."

The Captain let me finish but replied, "Well, I'm going to submit a policy change that the nanny has to live in your cabin."

The policy had to be reviewed by HR and I fought it. They called me into a meeting with several HR managers and the current Vice President of Entertainment who was a former Cruise Director. I remember their faces when I said, "You are challenging my leadership and my performance. I was in my cabin, sleeping with my baby when those alarms went off.

And I can tell you right now, half of your officers were in the crew bar until three in the morning, but you're judging me?"

The HR director looked at me and said, "You're really challenging this."

I said, "I'm sorry, but it's true. You criticize me, but yet if you walk in that officer bar, I'm pretty sure you're going to find some pretty high-level people who've had more than two drinks, and they're going to hear the alarm and have to go do their duty." I was just trying to open their minds, to show them how they were really putting me under the microscope but there was a bigger issue at hand. After that meeting, I am happy to say they let me do my job.

Despite the challenges, I remain proud that I was with a company that allowed me to be with my husband and my daughter.

There were many working moms who were guests cruising on the ship and one of them said something to me one night that really stuck with me. After I put on the first show, I would sit with Alanna on my lap to watch the next performance, and by this time she was singing every song. It was our special time together, as I worked all day, but it was my job to review the shows, and I could do this with my daughter in my lap. It was pure joy! And watching it through her eyes taught me so much about the guest experience.

This young woman said, "You know what, I'll be honest, in the beginning of the cruise, I didn't feel like I was connecting with you. Then, when I saw you with your daughter, I saw you in a whole different way. I thought you were just one of those young spokeswomen kind of person." Then she had a different impression of me. She saw me as a mom and a wife and also working and out there with the guests. It changed her perception. That was when I started to realize that it's okay to share the details of my life, that it's actually a good thing. So my fear eventually subsided, and I was really proud of what I was doing, although at the time, unconventional and very different. This made me grow as a leader and taught me to be more proactive, to stand up for myself and not be labeled by stereotypes.

It also opened my eyes to looking at diversity and other situations in a new light. You don't know how someone's feeling until you walk in their shoes. We all think we know how they feel, but it's one thing to tolerate it and it's another thing to accept it and then actually help them grow. We need to ask, "What do we need to do to make this better?"

WISDOM COMES FROM EXPERIENCE

For me, the coolest part about Kara's story from a company perspective is that even the largest companies on Earth have a first time for everything. No matter what size your company is, you have to figure out how to navigate many types of situations. There are global impacts if the company mishandles something like this; you could open yourself up to major lawsuits. Sometimes it's best to call in the experts to make sure you are making the right decisions.

It's eye opening to know that even international, world renowned companies were initiating new policies in real time while finding their way behind the scenes. Here's a first-person account of what happened in a major blue-chip company and how they treat mothers. That's monumental.

The company could easily have said, "This isn't going to work. What happens if there's an emergency?" They could have come up with any reason they wanted, but they took the chance. They took the position that they wanted to help this person because they realized her value and her talent and what she brought to the team.

SHIP TO SHORE

We can easily relate Kara's experience and company policies to a land-based or virtual business. Here's how:

- Do you have an existing maternity/paternity and family policy? If it is more than two years old, it is time to re-examine it.
- Don't just adapt an industry standard policy. Every workplace faces different challenges; customize to your work environment and be flexible and supportive to individual needs.
- Invite comment and then listen to what your employees need before you draft or update your policies. Is it flex time? Job sharing? Baby-changing rooms? Working from home?
- Do not hire the Octomom, it could bankrupt you.
- Remember, happy employees are more productive and your workplace will experience less turnover. Much like keeping a customer is a cost-saving measure, so is keeping good employees.

CHAPTER 13:

RUNNING A TIGHT SHIP: CREATING BOUNDARIES WITHIN YOUR ORGANIZATION

"TWO VALID FORMS OF ID, PLEASE." You hear this a lot. Maybe you are trying to lease a car, or you're applying for a driver's license in a new state. You are asked for ID all the time. Even if you don't drive, how many items do you have lying around with your name on them? That email you received from Ancestry.com probably didn't leap to mind, did it?

When you go on a cruise, you need to have an ID to get on board. For many years, you didn't need to have a passport for an American to cruise in the Caribbean; a birth certificate and a driver's license were sufficient. Some people have been saving up for years, and it is the first time they have ever left the shores of the United States, so it's not surprising they don't already have a passport. I recommend everyone apply for a passport, whether you have a trip planned or not. Passports are easy to get in six to eight weeks (or less if you pay to have it expedited), are universally accepted identification, plus, you never know when you might win a cruise!

You may be surprised when I tell you that the following story happened quite recently. Alvira came striding up to the check-in desk in the terminal in a flowing black and red maxi dress while her husband lagged several paces behind, in his white, short-sleeve oxford and powder blue trousers. When it came her turn to show ID before boarding, she reached into her satchel and pulled out, not her passport but, a sheaf of papers. In it were five sheets of neatly folded, eight-and-half-by-eleven inch sheets of paper she had printed off Ancestry.com, tracing her lineage back from Ohio, to Long Island, to Ellis Island to Italy, four generations ago.

She had not brought along a birth certificate, or even a library card. In her mind, her identity was far more verifiable than anyone boarding the ship that day, so you can imagine her surprise (indignation) when she was denied boarding. No amount of reasoning or cajoling on her part changed the outcome. The Pier Supervisor on duty that day felt terribly sorry for Alvira, and especially her husband whose face grew redder with every decibel as Alvira's voice rose, insisting we allow her to board. I could not make this ship up if I tried. But rules are rules, and they exist to keep people safe and to eliminate gray areas, making it more efficient for employees on the front line of customer service to make decisions.

The onboarding process for passengers is very precise and regimented. We travel to many countries and passport and visa requirements differ greatly among them. The complicated rules are spelled out in considerable detail for the crew to assure a passenger's trip is a smooth one wherever we dock. Every passenger passport is verified before they are allowed on board the ship.

Getting back to Alvira, less than a week later, the head office received a strongly worded letter from her, demanding a full refund and an apology from every crew member on board the ship that day, despite the fact that the website page she filled out to book the cruise clearly states the ID requirements. There are accountability markers included in the booking process that back up the policy. For instance, the reservations department was able to tell Alvira, "This is where you checked the box on June 9 that you read the policy. And here we can see that you opened the email, again with the written policy, on June 13."

Although it is never comfortable to deal with an unhappy customer, having very clear policies helps the staff make decisions on the spot, instead of having to make a judgment call on great-great-great-Uncle Luigi's bloodline.

Ninety-nine point nine percent of people follow the rules, but there's always that one exception, the one who makes you say your prayers to the Saint of HR Manuals. I think that's Saint Jude, the saint of lost causes.

Take shore excursions, for example. Cruise lines arrange all kinds of trips with third party organizers, from city tours to boat trips to exploring waterfalls and rain forests. There are a million things to do. All the details are on the ticket. I mean all the details. What time to meet the bus. Where to meet the bus. Do you need to bring a towel? Do you need to bring a raincoat, sunscreen, walking shoes, bottled water? Is lunch included? You name it. It's on that ticket. Then the staff gives guests verbal reminders as they depart. "Hold on to your ticket. That tells you when and where to meet your party."

We've had people show up thirty minutes late for their tour and ask why we didn't wait for them. "But our name is on the list!"

"Yes, your name is on the list, but do you want to tell Julie and Steve from New Jersey, and the 196 other people who made it on time for the tour, that they need to stand here and wait for *you*?"

It gets even more awkward when people return late to the bus. Are they just being rude, or are they injured? Did they have a medical emergency or just lose track of time, or maybe get lost? The policy is that the bus leaves with whoever is there, and again that's 99.9 percent of people. Then we track down the stragglers.

Even when it is the customer's fault for being late for a shore excursion, we still try to help them out. It is within our power to help them plan a nice day. We can offer them a later tour or tell them about some of the local treasures they can visit on their own.

Guest Services Managers (some cruise lines call them Front Desk Managers or Guest Relations Managers) are golden. No, that's an understatement. Each and every one of them is a saint. I could never do their job because all they do is deal with complaining or unhappy customers. No one will stand in line for fifteen minutes to approach the desk and say, "Hey, just dropping by to tell you, you're doing a bang-up job." Nope, they've waited fifteen minutes to unleash on someone. God bless the GSMs and their teams; they understand that it is not personal. They are there to lessen the pain and try to make things right, no matter who is to blame.

HEALTH AND SAFETY PROTOCOLS

Of course, there are rules—not just about customer service or local passport requirements—but also policies for health and safety.

A lot of health policies came about because of the outbreak of Legionnaires disease. The first known case occurred after a Philadelphia American Legion convention in 1976. In 1994, an outbreak occurred among passengers of a cruise ship who had used the Jacuzzi. Although there were more outbreaks in hotels than ships, the cruise industry was lumped into the bad press. The truth is, a cruise ship is safer and cleaner than a lot of other public environments because of stringent policies in place for decades. Now there are additional protocols for how often the chlorine is replenished, how often spas and pools are drained and cleaned, and a slew of other detailed procedures to keep everyone healthy. In some sense, this experience and ability to adapt quickly to threats is putting the cruise industry a step ahead. And after the coronavirus pandemic in 2020, health and safety protocols will again improve, with the cruise industry leading the way to keep customers and employees safe around the world.

Cruise lines treat all signs of illness seriously and have a level one, level two, and level three response, depending on the circumstances of what they are dealing with. All major cruise lines work closely with the Centers for Disease Control and Prevention to establish health and safety protocols, as well as mandatory reporting and compliance procedures. For example, if six or more guests come down with flu or norovirus symptoms in six hours, it triggers a response for a possible outbreak. If an outbreak reaches the next level of severity, then more procedures kick in, including increased sanitizing and less human-to-human contact around the ship. The ultimate goal is the health and safety of everyone on board, and cruise lines will go to great lengths to accomplish that objective.

DO PEOPLE REALLY FALL OVERBOARD?

I can assure you people do not just accidentally fall overboard. Either somebody is drunk, acting like a fool, or there is foul play involved. Ships are designed so that there is no way someone can accidentally tip over the side rails, which are approximately four feet high.

When alerted of a "man overboard" (women are included, I assure you), the bridge is immediately informed and told whether the person has gone over the port (left) or starboard (right) side. This makes all the difference in how the bridge slows and turns the ship to respond. As soon as the ship slows down, a very fast speedboat is lowered immediately, and goes out to search.

If a crew member witnesses someone going overboard, they throw them a life ring. These are spaced out all along the deck and help mark the spot. We can also throw a deck chair, which floats and also marks the spot, then they immediately call the bridge. There have been cases when someone did not return to their cabin and it went unnoticed until the next day. If it is deemed a man-overboard situation, the policy is to notify the Coast Guard (if we are close to the U.S.) and they assume the search and rescue operation.

And don't worry about those icebergs. Every cruise ship is required to have enough lifeboats and liferafts to evacuate 125 percent of the people on board. An extra lifeboat would have really come in handy when Jack and Rose were both trying to fit on that door in *Titanic*.

SHIP TO SHORE

The concepts we discussed in this chapter are based on sea stories, but you can easily convert them for use in your land-based or virtual business. Here's how:

- Once the rules are established, abide by them. If you are a manager and frequently bend the rules, you leave yourself open to constant negotiation from your team. If they see you are a consistent "by-the-book" person, they will come to you with fewer requests for exceptions. This also sets an example for them.

- Stand behind your employees when they are right. If you do have to make an exception to a policy, let the customer know it is a one-time allowance. And if your employee is wrong and you have to correct them, make sure you do it in private, never in front of the customer.

- Rules should not be arbitrary. They should establish an environment that keeps everyone safe, allowing them to perform their jobs to the best of their ability.

- Make new rules when necessary and get rid of the ones that no longer serve your business. If you haven't updated your policies and procedures or your HR manual in the last five years, what are you waiting for? For example, you can probably remove that rule about not distributing DVDs with 250 free hours of dial-up AOL on company time.

CHAPTER 14:

DECK CADETS: PLANNING FOR THE JUNIOR CRUISERS

"The greatest legacy we can leave our children is happy memories."
—Og Mandino

MAKING HAPPY MEMORIES is the driving force for the cruise industry and can be for your business, too. You don't have to be in the entertainment or vacation business to create positive and lasting memories for your customers. Accountants can make happy memories (tax return money). Dentists can make happy memories (new smile). Plumbers can make happy memories (hot water). When you are managing your business and planning your marketing, it is important to remember the children—for their sake and the sake of their parents and you. Let's break it down:

- Happy kids = happy parents.
- Kids are customers, too.
- Kids have strong brand loyalty and are expert negotiators.
- Children are your future customers.
- Kids drive their parents' purchasing decisions.
- An occupied, well-behaved child doesn't distract other customers.
- It costs less to convert a kid to a future customer than it does to win a new customer from a competitor.

THREE THINGS TO REMEMBER

When considering your youngest customers, remember:

+ Plan for the presence of children.
+ Don't assume you know what kids want.
+ Constantly retest, update, and redesign your strategy.

Remember that old TV show, *Kids Say the Darndest Things*? (It's actually back on the air with a new updated version.) Kids are little truth machines, so it's a good idea to listen to what they have to say. Not only will they crack you up with their candor, kids can guide your sales and marketing strategies, and save you money, too.

The cruise industry used to have the reputation of serving the sixty-five and up demographic. While we love that age group—they have the disposable income and the time to spend it—the industry wanted to expand the number and type of people they serve, which translates into *get more customers*. They did this by focusing on families. The success of Disney Cruise Line shows how successful this strategy is. It works for them and you can easily adapt it for your business, too.

Here are two important points that drive marketing strategy:

+ A 2018 Resonance Consultancy report states almost half of eighteen- to thirty-five-year-olds are traveling with kids.
+ Nearly two-thirds of parents with kids under five bring them along on trips.

You don't have to be in the vacation business to recognize the need for accommodating kids. If you are in a retail business, think about how many parents walk through your door with their kids in tow.

When I first started in the cruise industry back in the 1970s, the prevailing logic for the kids program was to put them in a room, let them play Dodgeball, and put a movie on TV. The Youth Staff only came on board seasonally, during the summer and over the Christmas and New Year's holidays. But now the programs have grown and grown and are year-round with special purpose rooms just for kids with the latest technology and games.

TALK TO THE KIDS

Cruise lines started by surveying the kids before spending millions of dollars on what they assumed kids wanted.

They formed focus groups with their existing customers and their kids and conducted exhaustive research. The kids were broken into age groups: three to five, six to eight, nine to eleven, twelve to fourteen, and fifteen to seventeen. The questions posed were mainly about what activities they would like on board. They received the usual responses from the smaller kids, but the most surprising reply came from the thirteen to seventeen-year-olds. I thought they would be interested in something to do with either the pool, rock climbing, or skateboarding. What do you think the number one response was when asked about what they were most interested in doing? Hang out. Yep, they just wanted to hang out with their friends.

Before investing millions on elaborate activities and equipment, and thanks to research, and just plain ol' asking them what they wanted, all they had to do was set aside some rooms with seating areas, a dance floor, and a sound system. They were open practically twenty-four hours a day (there is a curfew for kids and teens) with no parents allowed. We're not naive, so there was always one staff supervisor there. And these rooms were always close to the videogame room, which the teens loved as well.

This underscores the importance of the focus group, which we think is important to the customer. One of the major new renovations was the addition of water slides. Most of the mega-ships added slides on their newest, biggest ships and they were very successful, so now many lines are following suit, adding slides off the back of the ship. Not completely off the ship, although that could help reduce the line at the buffet.

Cruise lines are also adding laser tag, which is very popular with families. Not only do they want kid friendly activities, but also activities for the whole family. Laser tag is very big now on some ships and they're adding more and more. They may not be as popular in a few years, in which case the focus groups will be on top of the next trend and they'll replace laser tag with whatever that is.

There are educational programs as well. No, we aren't making the kids do math on their vacation—we want to create *happy* memories. Cruise lines have partnered with science and educational companies that provide all the supplies and guidance needed to lead kids in science experiments and other cool educational experiences. This is a good example of bringing in outside guidance for your company. You don't need to have specialized knowledge or equipment to add programs or bonuses for your customers. Chances are there are vendors who can add features on a trial basis, which will save you major investment dollars.

When cruise lines made the decision to target families, they knew they had to target kids because it would make them happy. And you know, the best comment we get at the end of the cruise is, "Oh, my kids didn't want to spend any time with us. They kept asking, 'When can we go back to the youth program?'"

Wouldn't you love to have an afternoon off while your kids go play with the counselors and you sit by the pool and have a nice drink or a nap? Or go enjoy a romantic meal, see a show, or try your luck in the casino while your kids enjoy a fully supervised program?

The whole kids program is so important because we know how important it is to the parents. Keeping the kids occupied and happy serves to eliminate any barrier to a family's successful cruise experience. Happy kids equal happy parents.

When I meet with a youth team, I let them know how important their work is, because when they first start out, they may be under the impression that kids' activities aren't valued as much as those for adults.

A GOOD KIDS PROGRAM IS A WIN-WIN-WIN

The kids win because they have something fun and age-appropriate to do.

The parents win because they get time to be adults and relax.

The cruise line wins because they are increasing their customer base and laying the groundwork for future customers, which means increased revenue.

And here's one more group to consider: The people without kids win, too. If you are someone without children, or on a kid-free getaway, the last thing you want is to be annoyed with other people's noisy or disruptive kids.

SPECIAL KID GROUPS

Taking care of the kids isn't always about keeping the passengers happy and boosting revenue. At the heart of it, your strategy for kids really needs to be about compassion and serving the needs of children. When you think about it, kids don't have that much control over their own lives. They rely on the adults around them for everything: food, safety, shelter, education, and quality of life.

Some of the cruise lines I've worked with have hosted different types of kid groups, including those with autism, the hearing impaired and Down's Syndrome. These have been some of the most satisfying and rewarding cruises I have done. We've also had many Make-A-Wish® families join us over the years and those cruises also hold a special place in my heart. If you are not familiar with Make-A-Wish® International, they are an international nonprofit organization that makes wishes come true for critically ill children. They create joyful experiences for children in nearly fifty countries. Children's wishes are usually pretty simple and include wanting a puppy or a PlayStation or meeting a celebrity—and every now and then going on a cruise. By making these easily obtainable dreams come true, ninety-seven percent of Wish parents say that their child's emotional health was improved. And we all know how important attitude is toward healing. We send families a questionnaire in advance so we can make each child's trip everything they've dreamed of. We ask about their favorite foods. We ask if they would like to tour the bridge and meet the Captain. Would they like to be introduced from the stage? We take steps to know everything we can about a child's likes and dislikes before they board.

HOW YOUR BUSINESS CAN BENEFIT FROM KIDS

Let's take a moment to brainstorm how other businesses can benefit from any sort of kid accommodations—anything from short-term day care to organized activities. The key here is to plan ahead. It doesn't mean keeping some lollipops in your desk drawer to hand out.

Start by analyzing how long parents spend in your place of business and what they are doing while they are there.

If customers are in your establishment for short periods of time, something as simple as making sure your reception areas are child proof reduces stress for everybody. Take a look around your lobby. Do you have sharp edges or glass sculptures within reach of little hands? If so, move these items out of their reach. Kids are like alligators; you really shouldn't turn your back on them.

Gyms and health clubs can keep parents coming in the door with kid-focused activities. This could range from kids yoga to supervised swimming exercises. Think beyond babysitting. Anything educational is a value-add.

Children should not be an afterthought. Plan for them ahead of time. You're creating customer loyalty. If parents know there is a supervised play area at your business, you can have an edge over the competition.

SHIP TO SHORE

Let's take the lessons learned and apply them to your business. Are you **really considering everything that can make your customer's experience exceptional?** To make the starting line perfect, you have to consider the person coming in your door and who's coming with them, because that's a huge part of their experience. Here's how:

- Kids are customers too. They are a source of revenue today *and* down the road.
- Kids are not an afterthought. Start planning for them right away.
- Don't underestimate how much a child can influence a parent's buying decisions. (That's why grocery stores place candy bars at eye level to kids in the checkout line. This will give the kids maximum time to whine and beg and annoy their parents into purchasing it. It's a proven money maker. These grocery store executives have done their homework.)
- Safety and fun are equally important.
- Keeping the kids entertained benefits everybody.

CHAPTER 15:

A RISING TIDE LIFTS ALL BOATS: EMPOWERING YOUR TEAM

FUN FACT: "A RISING TIDE LIFTS ALL BOATS" is an aphorism frequently attributed to John F. Kennedy. Oh, how often we forget that every president since Warren G. Harding in 1921 had a speech writer. According to Ted Sorensen, Kennedy's speechwriter, "a rising tide lifts all boats" was the slogan of The New England Council Chamber of Commerce, and he thought it was particularly apt to use in Kennedy's 1963 speech defending a dam project. It describes how improvements in the general economy benefit all the members of that economy.

Much in the same way, empowering team members benefits the economic health of the entire company. In previous chapters we talked about the rules. Now let's put some of them to work. With solid policies and procedures in place, and a highly trained team you trust, you are on your way to increasing customer satisfaction and, by correlation, boosting your bottom line.

There will be complaints. You can have the best product, best service, best employees this side of the pearly gates, and someone will complain. Orders will be wrong, food will be cold, buses will be late, entertainers will hit flat notes. And you will be ready.

In his book *The 4-Hour Workweek*, author Tim Ferris tells a story about a discovery he made back in 2004. He was in a decision-bottleneck in his sports nutrition business, so he empowered his assistants to make hundred-dollar fixes. Ferris recognized he was spending twenty to thirty hours a week answering questions about fulfillment and customer service, not generating new business.

It was taking days to respond to low dollar problems. Clearly not a man with control issues, Ferris decided to empower his employees. He gave his assistants the power to make decisions and offer solutions that cost $100 or less. They were to document the decision in a spreadsheet he would review at the end of the week. He then reviewed them every two weeks, then every month, then every quarter. The process was so successful he raised the decision ceiling to $1,000. He placed trust in his team, increased customer satisfaction, and freed up his time to go make more money and host podcasts.

EMPOWER YOUR EMPLOYEES

One of the most frequent customer complaints is repeating themselves over and over again when they have a problem. They have to retell their story to every person they get handed off to. It can take ten times longer to go through a chain of command to fix the problem when it can be fixed immediately simply by empowering your front-line team members. Additionally, customer satisfaction surveys speak to this and usually includes the question: Was your complaint addressed in a timely manner? Was it handled the first time? Empowering your employees to handle concerns and complaints immediately ensures greater customer satisfaction as well as increased employee engagement.

And what about those reviews? Did you know there is actually a good-to-bad review ratio? According to the magazine *Inc.*, one bad review needs forty good ones to offset it.

A HAPPY CUSTOMER IS A REPEAT CUSTOMER

A happy, satisfied passenger will book their next cruise while they are still on board, which is the goal of every cruise line. It's an emotional decision based on the current, positive experience. A negative experience can drive them right to the competition. Furthermore, nearly half of consumers say the recommendations of friends or family members influence them. A happy customer not only becomes a repeat customer, but brings new customers as well, with no additional marketing cost.

Harvard research has shown that a five percent increase in retention can boost profits upward of ninety-five percent. We want that customer back. Now how can we make that happen? By making them happy right now. And it's easier than you think. In the cruise industry, we started with a bottle of wine. We empowered our customer service employees to offer a bottle of wine to unhappy customers and it worked like a charm. Instead of spending the rest of the cruise cranky and unhappy, these customers were satisfied, and in some cases, tipsy. Their dissatisfaction period was reduced from weeks to minutes for a ten-dollar (usually less) bottle of wine.

Unfortunately, this practice was too successful, as guests started telling other guests all they had to do to get a free bottle of wine was go to the front desk and complain about something. The policy was eventually revised and updated, and now there is more wine to actually sell. Of course, depending on your business, wine is not always the appropriate answer. It can be a gift card or a voucher for a future service. Focus on future business. When the customer is happy they are more likely to return. This is something restaurants do all the time. Think of birthday club rewards. They know in order to use that free appetizer certificate people are likely to return and bring at least three friends with them. Depending on the restaurant, this translates to a sixty- to seventy-dollar sale for a five-dollar expense.

If the problem cannot be solved on the spot, don't string people along. If you say, "I'm going to research it and get back to you tomorrow by email," then you better get back to them tomorrow. Even if you don't have an answer, you email them and say, "I'm still working on it; I haven't forgotten about you. Give me another day please." Integrity is priceless, so keep your word. Otherwise the customer may say, "You know what? Forget this; I'm going down the road to your competitor."

PUTTIN' ON THE RITZ

One of the most famous examples of the customer service empowerment scenario is Ritz-Carlton hotels. Their motto is, "We are Ladies and Gentlemen serving Ladies and Gentlemen." They even spell out their credo, motto, and service values (a commitment to clients and employees) on their website.

Every Ritz-Carlton employee is empowered to use up to $2,000 of company funds to please a guest. This spend doesn't necessarily have to be used to address an issue of dissatisfaction. Those little extras, a room upgrade, ordering your dinner for you in Mandarin, giving directions to an Uber driver, can result in a return customer for life. And the widely publicized stories are worth more than hundreds of thousands of advertising dollars. (There is a story about a chef in a Bali resort who asked his mother-in-law to fly in with specialized eggs and milk for a child with food allergies.)

Not only do they encourage employees to solve problems and support them in going the extra mile for the client, they implement solutions worldwide across their brand with something they call the innovation database. When a new strategy has proven successful, it is entered into the database for properties throughout the chain to adopt. Cruise lines also use this strategy by keeping a "best practices" file that all ships can share and learn from others' experiences, whether it is a new port of call, new recipes that are successful, or new onboard innovations. Empowering employees to solve problems on their own builds trust among team members.

It also increases employee engagement. According to *Forbes*, "The Gallup organization reminds us every couple of years that nearly seventy percent of employees are actively disengaged." That is not good. Employees want to know their voice matters and that they can be part of the solution.

It comes down to attitude. You can choose to think, "There's no way we're going to get past this problem; let's not even think of a solution." Or you can adopt the view that every problem has a solution. We just might not have thought of it yet. It may not come up today or tomorrow; it might come up next week or a year from now, but every problem has a solution.

SHIP TO SHORE

The lessons from these stories can easily be applied in a land-based or virtual business. Here's how:

- When deciding how to handle a customer complaint, remember it costs seven to ten times more to gain a customer than to keep one. Make it a win-win for everyone.
- Referring to a complaining customer as "Ace" or "Chief" or "Buckaroo" is a terrible move, unless of course it's your last day on the job, in which case have at it and go out in a blaze of glory!
- Extend trust to your staff and you will be rewarded with increased employee satisfaction and better customer service.
- No-cost and low-cost solutions can both assure customer loyalty and empower your team.
- Perspective is everything . . . the sinking of the *Titanic* was a miracle to the lobsters in the kitchen.

CHAPTER 16:

BETWEEN THE DEVIL
AND THE DEEP BLUE SEA

IF IT CAN HAPPEN on land, it can happen at sea. Life's daily dramas don't stop at the gangway. Human nature doesn't change, and proclivities don't get left on the dock. What can I say? Sometimes our guests are naughty. Sometimes they're downright murderous. One thing I *can* say is our guests are also very loyal.

Most cruise lines have a loyalty program, and each program has different tiers, depending on how many cruises (or nights in some cases) you have spent on board. And in all cases, it can be difficult to reach the top tier. For some lines, you have to spend the equivalent of around a hundred seven-day cruises to reach the top level. The top tier for Holland America Line is called the 5-Star Mariner; for Celebrity Cruises the top level is Zenith; for Norwegian Cruise Line it is the Ambassador level; and for Royal Caribbean International the top tier is Pinnacle Club. Once you reach the highest level, the benefits can be quite nice. Depending on the line, the perks for the top tier can include dinner in the specialty restaurants, free bottles of wine, free internet, and even free cruises.

As you can imagine, there are very few guests at these top levels, as it takes time and money to get there. Some of the members of these top tiers like to wear their membership proudly. They enjoy their status and the fact they are part of an exclusive group. They have their own pin and wear it with pride. Some of them are a little snobby and walk around like they own the place. But most of them are just the most wonderful people in the world and very down-to-earth; you'd never know they were part of the top level.

I had been with Royal Caribbean for quite some time and got to know some of the Pinnacle Club members well, since they sailed so often. Pinnacle members can drink for free for a few hours each night in Members Only lounges. It's one of the perks they get for their loyalty. They love their free drinks and will take advantage of this popular benefit. I would too. Free booze!

One evening some of the Pinnacle members were getting pretty drunk in the lounge. Two couples, actually. Let's call them Bob and Carol and Ted and Alice. Everybody knew these people. The crew all knew these people because they have sailed with us so often.

You know how liquor makes everything hilarious? You know how liquor makes people lose their inhibitions? You know how rational decision-making is skewed by drinking?

For some unknown alcohol-infused reason, Bob bet Ted a hundred bucks that he wouldn't go behind the bar and drop his pants.

So, what does Ted do? He goes behind the bar and he drops his pants in front of the female bartender. This is completely unacceptable. The two couples are asked to leave; the guys are completely mystified by this reaction. After all, they are Pinnacle Club members. They think the whole thing is hilarious. But poor Alice, Ted's wife, was absolutely humiliated and couldn't make her way out of the bar fast enough, which was tragically difficult as she was slowed down by her walker. This also gives you some idea as to the age of the saggy, flabby rear end that the poor bartender was forced to see.

The bartender made an official complaint, as well she should. This was completely over the line, Pinnacle member or not. Within hours the complaint reached the Captain, who reviewed the video tapes. There are cameras everywhere on board, and cameras from two different angles caught the entire incident. The Captain called the two couples into his office and said, "It's right here on the tape, and if you think I'm going to take your word over my crew member, you are sadly mistaken." Then he ordered the two couples off the ship at the next port of call. Now this is a Pinnacle member, one of our top cruisers, who has spent hundreds of thousands of dollars with us, and the Captain didn't hesitate to give them the heave ho (OK, I couldn't resist the nautical term for hauling rope. What do you expect after forty years at sea?)

Many, if not all cruise lines, have a guest conduct policy that addresses unacceptable onboard behavior. Part of this policy addresses harassing the crew, and this guy was in clear violation. The Captain said, "That's obviously harassment," sent the issue to the head office, who agreed and banned the couple from ever cruising with the line.

The Captain got big props from all the crew members. Everything gets around the ship. Everybody talks and knows everybody else's business. Think about the loyalty that he earned from that action.

The customer is NOT always right. No matter how much money a customer spends, rules and decency should prevail.

SOME PEOPLE ARE IDIOTS

I would like to assure you again that no one ever falls overboard by accident. They jump or they are pushed, and in one case, some fool had his friend videotape him jumping from his balcony into the water while we were docked. The blockbuster *Titanic* did not do the cruise industry any favors. We've had a few people try to reenact the King of the World scene on the bow of the ship. It does not end well. And the guy who posted his balcony stunt on social media? Cruise lines are on social media too and saw it right away. They threw him off the ship immediately and told him to find his own way home. They also banned him for life.

WHEN THERE'S FOUL PLAY

At times, I've felt like I've woken up in the middle of a *Lifetime* movie. Chip and Chelsea were a noticeable couple—young, attractive, well-dressed, and gregarious. Far from being wrapped up only with each other on their honeymoon cruise, by day two, they had made plenty of shipboard friends. In the early morning hours of day five, Chelsea was found passed out in a hallway on the other side of the ship from their cabin. Chip was never seen again.

Dozens of witness statements tell conflicting stories of what happened the night before, but some facts remain consistent: Chelsea has no memory of anything prior to dinner time the previous evening. Witnesses heard the loud voices of several men in their cabin at around 4:00 in the morning. Guests in neighboring cabins recount the sound of thuds, scraping balcony furniture, and slamming doors at about the same time. Bloody handprints were discovered on the lifeboat canopy two decks below Chelsea and Chip's cabin.

From what the crew pieced together on the shipboard grapevine, Chip and Chelsea wore their wealth openly. Chip flashed his expensive watch and you could see Chelsea's massive engagement ring across the casino floor, where some say they boasted of how much wedding cash they had tucked away in their cabin.

Both were last seen together partying with four men in the disco at around 3:00 a.m. One guest reported that both were a little tipsy at around 2:30 a.m., but by 3:00 a.m., neither one could walk without assistance. Such a rapid descent into weakness and confusion is consistent with being roofied (having a drug slipped into your drink).

Port police, and later the FBI, extensively questioned the four men last seen with Chip. The crew already knew them as unruly and belligerent. Three days later, their continued bad behavior along with other passenger complaints got them kicked off the ship.

After years of stateside investigation, no one has ever discovered the complete story of that night, but investigators are getting closer to the truth after an incriminating video surfaced of the three men bragging about their part in Chip's death. In an ironic twist, one of the men was later found murdered in his own driveway.

Once again, you can't make this ship up. It only seemed natural to name this chapter "Between the Devil and the Deep Blue Sea," a song written in 1931 and recorded by many artists since then, including Ella Fitzgerald and George Harrison.

> I want to cross you off my list
> But when you come knocking at my door
> Fate seems to give my heart a twist
> And I come running back for more
> I should hate you but I guess I love you
> You got me in between the devil and the deep blue sea

I love the cruise industry. Despite the challenges of life at sea, spending months away from home, and the occasional melodrama, I keep coming back for more.

SHIP TO SHORE

What takeaways from this chapter can be applied to your land-based business?

- If you need rules for your guests or customers, post them publicly.
- Gently but insistently enforce the rules.
- Your customer is with you an hour or a day or a week, but a good employee will be with you for years. They deserve your support.
- Trust me, you are drunker than you think you are.
- The above note is not nearly as funny as it was when you were in college.

CHAPTER 17:

WHATEVER FLOATS YOUR BOAT: KEEPING THE CUSTOMER HAPPY

THE CRUISE INDUSTRY has always looked for ways to amaze their guests. Most of the things that can make people happy don't have to cost a lot or take a lot of time.

Years ago, there was a country song called "Satin Sheets" by Jeannie Pruett. From the minute Miss Barbara heard that song as a teenager she wanted satin sheets. As she got older and got a job and money of her own, she always put satin sheets on her bed. Miss Barbara got married and divorced, and the satin sheets became deeply symbolic for her because of the lyrics, "Satin sheets to lie on, satin pillows to cry on, Still, I'm not happy don't you see."

So it stands to reason that when Barbara took her post-divorce cruise with us, with her settlement money, she would want satin sheets. Now we have very nice sheets and comforters and pillows. People like them so much, they're for sale on board. But Barbara wanted satin sheets. She insisted on them, actually.

The Hotel Director decided that he would send somebody out at the first port of call to find some satin sheets for Miss Barbara. He called ahead to the port agent, who lives on the island, and he went out to the local stores and purchased some satin sheets. When we docked, the agent brought them on board and Miss Barbara was thrilled. She had her special satin sheets for the rest of her cruise.

Because we fulfilled her request, she booked two more future cruises while still on board. It's this willingness to go above and beyond and come up with creative solutions that ensure repeat customers.

KEEPING IT CLEAN

I was working on a ship out of Baltimore, Maryland, and it's very common for people who board in Baltimore to stay with us for many months during the winter. These guests live around that whole Washington, D.C., Virginia, Maryland, Delaware, West Virginia corridor. To escape the cold and ice during the winter months, they have a choice: They can rent or buy a house in Florida, like many people do and be a snowbird during the winter months. For some people, though, it's cheaper to book a cruise for four months than to rent a house, rent a car, go out and buy food, cook the food, drive around, and so on and so forth. Everything's right there for you on a cruise, including a full medical facility in case you need it.

Some people will come on for three or four cruises, then go home and do their laundry, then maybe come back for three or four cruises. Eleanor stayed on board for four months and only had one request. Could we wash her laundry separately? She needed her clothes washed a certain way because the detergent that we were using caused her to get a rash. So, she brought her own detergent with her, and the laundry team did her laundry separately using her own detergent.

Those are just some of the things we'll do to keep people happy. It's all about the little things that generate repeat customers with their referrals and recommendations.

THE NAKED TRUTH

As much as you try to anticipate the needs of your clients, and as many ways as you devise to entertain them, your imagination will never match theirs. We like to have an open mind to suggestions, requests, and special bookings because our goal is to create unforgettable experiences.

You may have heard people say that if you are nervous about speaking in front of a group of people, just imagine them naked. For some reason, that is supposed to make you less nervous.

But what if the audience you are speaking to is *actually* naked? Seriously. Like TOTALLY NAKED!

I was fortunate (?) enough to be the Cruise Director on board a Costa Cruise Line ship for a seven-day, clothing-optional cruise. That's right. The entire ship, over 2,000 people, were allowed to be TOTALLY NAKED from the time we reached the twelve-mile limit outside of port, and most of them were. (I'm not sure why I keep capitalizing TOTALLY NAKED; it just seems right.)

Now before I tell you about this cruise, let me tell you about full ship charters. We love them. A business or travel partner books the entire ship for a theme cruise or business incentive meeting. They purchase every room on board, and then they are responsible for filling the ship, either by selling tickets or giving away staterooms to their top producers, vendors, friends, etc. We will change the itinerary for them, enhance the menu with special items, or bring on entertainers they would like to see. We will do whatever it takes to please them, as they pretty much "own" the ship for those seven days.

The more common types of full ship charters are music cruises (jazz, pop, rock and roll, oldies, gospel, Elvis impersonators) that feature some of your favorite artists performing during the cruise.

There are sports charters, where a professional or college sports team will bring on some of their current and former players and coaches and hold autograph and speaker sessions for their fans.

There are cruises for people with health concerns (hearing impaired, autistic), different lifestyles (LGBTQ), or religious cruises. Take your pick, we've had them all! One of my most memorable cruises was a full ship scientific charter that followed a total eclipse of the sun. It was an unforgettable experience with wonderful memories and incredible photos.

And then there are the business charters for a big national or international company that will charter the ship for a cruise to have their yearly meetings on board, invite their senior executives and top producers, along with their significant others, have a wonderful time in various ports—then write the whole thing off as a tax deduction!

Now this particular full ship charter cruise was clothing-optional. Once the ship left port and was twelve miles out, the clothes came off. Now let me tell you up front, there were certain rules, regulations, and etiquette. For example, it is common in the clothing-optional world that everyone sits on towels. No one ever sits directly on any furniture or chair, as that is considered improper, unhealthy, and uncivilized. (And any other word you want to think of, like "gross.") So, we had loads of clean towels all around the ship, always being replenished. The only place clothes were mandatory was the main dining room (but not the upstairs or poolside buffet) and at the Captain's Welcome Aboard Cocktail Party where picture taken with the Captain. But everywhere else, you were on your own.

In case you were wondering, the crew was not naked. (Insert your own joke or sigh of relief here.) And if the crew felt at all uncomfortable being in this environment (remember we have crew from all over the world with many different cultural upbringings), they had the option to transfer to another ship for this particular cruise.

The key to making sure this was a successful cruise was communication. We knew close to a year in advance about this cruise, and as you can imagine, it was the thing just about everyone was talking about on board. We met with representatives from the travel agency putting the cruise together many times in advance to talk about pretty much everything. The playbook was large and detailed. We were fortunate the agency had done this successfully many times in the past on other cruise lines. Therefore, while it was new to us, it was anything but new to them. They had answers to all of our questions, which helped put us at ease.

One thing I learned very quickly during the cruise was how to hold and maintain eye contact. How could you not have wandering eyes at first when there are naked people all around you, but it was something I tried really hard to master. It was not easy. Not everyone got naked. Which was a shame, because some of the people you wanted to see naked for some reason kept their clothes on.

These were some of the nicest people I had ever sailed with, and I wanted to have conversations with them throughout the cruise. As Cruise Director, I was expected to socialize. I had wonderful talks with people from all walks of life, from corporate CEOs to military personnel, they were all on board, and TOTALLY NAKED! They were open and frank about their lifestyle, and I have to think those guests were used to wandering eyes.

Many guests were there because it was a chance to get away and live out a fantasy without family or friends knowing about it. Some guests mentioned no one in their families knew about their secret escapades.

Yes, in case you were wondering, we had naked Bingo! (You were wondering, weren't you?) It was not your average Bingo session, I can assure you. But it's nice to know that everyone still gets excited when they win money! (Don't ask me how I could tell.)

Ironically, there was a masquerade party on this cruise, where they actually put clothes on, and it was unbelievable. Some people had worked on their costumes all year. Some had questionable themes we can't discuss here in public, but use your wildest imagination, and then double it. I was lucky enough to host it, and the Captain, Hotel Director and Chief Engineer were the judges. Usually, an activity like this will last an hour. With so many people participating, this one took well over three hours! I have pictures, but I'm not supposed to have pictures, so I can't show you. Sorry.

This cruise sold out immediately, and there was a long waiting list! Which means this lifestyle is quite popular, and these cruises commanded top dollar. This was the twenty-fifth time this travel group had chartered a ship for a clothing-optional cruise. They were very successful in carving out a very small piece of the pie and delivering what their customers wanted.

The cruise was successful because they were so organized. Everyone from the executives down to all employees, crew, and guests were kept informed about all happenings, policies, and procedures. Nothing was left to chance, from the menus to the activities and entertainment.

Communication was key in all forms, from written to verbal. Everyone was on the same page. Of course, there were things that went wrong during the cruise, but because everything was so well planned, they remained minor hiccups and not huge challenges. The key was starting early, learning from past mistakes, and being open to new ideas.

And keep your eyes from wandering.

MY TRAVEL AGENT TOLD ME

If I had a dime for every time someone came up to me and said, "My travel agent told me ..."

"My travel agent told me there are free drinks in the casino." No sir, that's Las Vegas where they have huge casinos, thousands of slot machines, hundreds of gaming tables and they're making millions of dollars a night." We have a small casino that doesn't compare, so no, we don't have free drinks in the casino.

"My travel agent told me that all I had to do was ask and I'd get a free upgrade to a room with a balcony." The balcony cabins always fill up first, so all of those staterooms are booked. On the rare occasion one is available, cruise lines will charge for the upgrade.

A few people have said, "I'm a stockholder in your company. I want an upgraded stateroom." Our response, "As a stockholder, you want us to make as much money as possible, don't you? That's why you invested your hard-earned cash with our company, right? If we were to give cabins away, like you're asking, well, then you wouldn't be happy with the stock price because we wouldn't be making all the money we could. So as a stockholder, you should be happy that we're charging for upgrades." That pretty much puts the end to that conversation.

There are limits to how much service anyone can provide. On one cruise, a guy walked up to me and handed me his two-month old baby saying, "My travel agent told me you have free babysitting all cruise long." He thought we had free babysitting twenty-four-hours a day and he just gave me his baby and said, "Here, I'll see you in a week." I'm not sure where the mother was when this happened. (Okay, he didn't really hand me his baby, it just sounded more dramatic that way.)

I told him that unfortunately he was misinformed. We have babysitting on board, but not twenty-four hours a day, seven days a week. I then asked him, "Could I get the name of your travel agent so we can tell them that they're giving out wrong information?"

And all of a sudden it was, "Well, no, I don't really want to give you the name of the travel agency. I don't want to get them in trouble."

I replied, "If they are giving out wrong information, we need to know about it, so we can set the record straight and make sure they give out accurate information."

I actually happened to have a brochure right near me and showed it to him saying, "Just so you know, this is our policy right here in black and white. Every travel agent has this."

We worked out an arrangement where I was able to get him a babysitter on the two formal nights so that he and his wife could have a nice dinner and see a show. And I picked up the tab for the babysitting. We had a miscellaneous account that we could draw from for certain things like that. Ultimately, we were able to take care of the problem, partway. He was happy with what we worked out. It turned out he's a graduate of Boston University and I'm a graduate of Boston University. By the end of the cruise, he was my best friend. But the fact is he came on board with certain expectations that we couldn't meet, but we worked out a solution that was agreeable to all.

I should mention we know Travel Agents don't say all these things to guests. They know better. We love Travel Agents; they are so important to the travel industry.

FROM THE CRADLE TO THE GRAVE

From babysitting to burials at sea, the cruise industry's got you covered. What better way to honor a loved one than by giving them a beautiful, peaceful send off? One final cruise. Our burials at sea are for cremated remains, not shroud covered corpses like you see in the movies. The family will notify us when they book a cruise and we make arrangements for a small, dignified ceremony. Usually the Staff Captain and the Chief Safety Officer are present with the family at the sunrise service. They check the wind speed and slow the ship down so the family can spread the cremains off the back of the ship with the ashes going aft. And yes, it's already in my will. What a way to go.

SHIP TO SHORE

While you may not be entertaining naked people, let's see if there are some takeaways for your land-based business.

- Is the cost of what your customer is asking less than what a bad review would cost you? Consider the repeat business you could get from this client by acceding to their request.
- Don't just say no. Train your staff to be open-minded to requests and negotiate win-wins.
- The customer is not always right. The customer always *thinks* they're right. And they are always the customer. Treat them

with the respect they deserve. Try to make every situation a win-win, where no one walks away the loser. It will serve you well in the long run.

- If you're booked to go on a naked cruise, make sure Judy from accounting is not on the manifest. That could be quite awkward, and we all know she's nuts.

CHAPTER 18:

LIKE WATER OFF A DUCK'S BACK: HANDLING CRITICISM IN THE SOCIAL MEDIA AGE

"The trouble with most of us is that we would rather be ruined by praise than saved by criticism."
—Dr. Norman Vincent Peale

CRITICISM IS NOT EASY for any of us to take. So much of it stems from misunderstanding, jealousy, or just plain cruelty. But true critique is an opportunity to learn and improve.

Let's be honest. Does anyone really like or want feedback? Especially when it's negative or vindictive? Of course not.

We definitely want to hear positive feedback; that makes us feel good and feeds our ego. We enjoy hearing when someone appreciates our product or service. But negative feedback—no thanks.

Every business should want as much feedback as possible—the good, the bad, and especially the ugly. Bill Gates once said, "We all need people who will give us feedback. That's how we improve." And also, "It's fine to celebrate success, but it is more important to heed the lessons of failure." His comments stress the importance of learning from your mistakes. And I guess you can say he is somewhat of a success.

Feedback in the cruise industry is vital to improving. And we get a lot of it. Every month, every week, every day. As Cruise Director I am front and center hosting all the main entertainment on stage and the big activities around the ship, so suffice it to say I have received my fair share of feedback, both positive and negative. That is one of the drawbacks about living with your customers ... they are right there to tell you how they feel.

At the end of every cruise, we asked our guests for their feedback on the surveys that we provided in their staterooms. Up until around 2012, most cruise lines offered paper surveys in the cabins on the last day of the cruise; they filled them out and deposited in a locked collection box at the front desk. After the cruise ended, the surveys were sent to our head office where they were scanned, tabulated, and reviewed. Unfortunately, this process took a week, so it wasn't a very efficient system.

There was no time to correct any mistakes that could have led to a better review. For instance, if we were to see a number of complaints that the mashed potatoes were horrible, we could take them off the buffet right away instead of serving them every night.

We know that having more surveys returned to us means more accurate feedback and better ideas for improvement. You get a much better picture from a thousand surveys than you do from ten surveys. If four out of ten people didn't like the mashed potatoes it seems significant. If four out of a thousand people didn't like the mashed potatoes, well, they're just not potato people.

To encourage our guests to fill out the survey we told them we'd enter everyone who did into a drawing for a free cruise. Wow, right?! We saw after a brief period that this was skewing our results in several ways. In order to win, we of course needed to know the person's name. This means that their response is not anonymous. People thought if they said anything negative, they wouldn't win the free trip. This resulted in under reporting of valid criticism. Suddenly those crappy mashed potatoes don't matter so much with a free trip on the line.

After 2012, cruise lines started using technology to email guests a link to an online survey at the end of the trip and give them one week to respond. No need for those locked wooden boxes and the cruise incentive.

The first question we asked was, "Overall, how well did you enjoy your vacation?" In addition, our guests are asked to rate areas around the ship, such as food, stateroom, entertainment, service, etc. with a numerical score of one through ten or a satisfaction score (excellent, good, fair, poor).

The most important question on the survey is, "On a scale of one to ten (one being the lowest, ten the highest), how likely are you to recommend us to your family and friends?" I'm sure you have seen this question on surveys you have filled out. Each score is tabulated, and the end result is called the Net Promoter Score, or NPS.

NPS basically tells your company whether or not a customer will return and use your services again, and more importantly, refer you to family, friends, and neighbors. Every business should want to know this important indicator. There is a lot of debate in the business world about NPS scores; some companies use them religiously, others think it is not a good tool, but the bottom line is that every company should want their customers to be raving brand ambassadors. To sing your praises. It is important to find out if the product or service you deliver is worthy of someone recommending you to family and friends, because those are the most important recommendations. As a consumer, you're never really sure who is leaving anonymous reviews online, but you should always be able to trust the recommendations from your family and friends.

After we receive the scores for the various areas around the ship, next comes the second and best part of the survey. The comment section. Oh, do we love the comment section (he said sarcastically). In the early years with the paper comment cards, there were only a few lines for comments, so people didn't write that much, but when the surveys moved online and they had a week to think about it and unlimited space to write, we started receiving a lot more feedback. Our guests do not hold back. Man they do not hold back! And that is okay with us. We want to hear what they have to say. We want to improve.

We've all received negative comments from time to time, and some of them are hard to swallow. One of my most memorable was,

"Throw Paul the Cruise Director overboard and drag him behind the ship."

Ouch! That one stung a bit, but it's okay, I like the water. I always thought I was a nice guy, so reading that comment hurt. I'm only human, and we all have a bit of an ego, so I really tried to figure out what I could have possibly done to earn this negative review. But that's a losing battle. Constructive comments are welcomed, vindictive comments serve no purpose. Maybe it was the potatoes.

Fortunately, the positive comments ("very professional," "loved that he was approachable and always had time to talk," "Paul helped us solve a family emergency with compassion and empathy"), far outweigh the negative ones, or else I wouldn't have lasted so long. And I learned early on to have thick skin.

If you're a leader, manager, or supervisor out there, remember that positive reinforcement is important for your team. We all like to get a pat on the back every once in a while. Please remember, share positive comments and results publicly, but keep those negative comments behind closed doors. You never want to shame anyone and broadcast negative feedback. As legendary football coach Vince Lombardi once said, "Praise in public, criticize in private."

We also learned that ninety-eight percent of our customers were wonderful people who loved our product. But we thought it was important to try and convert those remaining two percent who weren't happy. That was a mistake. We learned those two percent are never happy; they're always miserable about something in their lives, and nothing we could do would ever make them happy. So we decided to make sure we kept the other ninety-eight percent happy and motivated to come back.

You can learn a lot from thoughtful, constructive comments. Look for trends. If a team member gets a one-off comment, that might not be anything to worry about, but if that person gets the same negative comment over and over, such as they were rude, or they showed up late, then there is a problem that needs to be addressed with more training and coaching. Repeated negative comments week after week are a red flag.

Statistics tell us (we love statistics, don't we?) that only four percent of people who have a problem with your product or service will actually tell you. The other ninety-six percent just walk away, never to be seen again. So if your customer is taking the time to tell you about a problem … LISTEN! These people will do business with you again if you fix the problem right the first time and in a timely manner.

Reading negative comments can be difficult. But realize your customers are giving you a gift by taking the time to let you know about their experience. Thank them for it, fix the problem, show your appreciation and they will be back.

BUT I READ IT ON THE INTERNET

In addition to your company-generated reviews, there are countless online forums and websites devoted to customer reviews. Yelp reviews. Google reviews. Amazon reviews. There are also industry-specific review sites for restaurants, colleges, wedding planners, doctors, and of course the cruise industry. While we monitor all online mentions, it is important to separate useful critique from the ranting customers (they are not all named Karen) of this world. Below are a few of the comments floating around out there about me.

"Paul needs to retire."

"Paul is one of my favorites and always has been."

"Perfect comedic timing."

"Overall lack of energy."

"Not pushy or over the top. Enjoyed his laid back style."

Everyone's opinion is different. When you read all the social media commentary it can sometimes seem like a retelling of *The Three Little Bears*. I may be the worst, I may be the best, but apparently my timing is "just right."

You are never as good as your best reviews and never as bad as your worst reviews.

Although my comedic timing *is* perfect.

DO YOUR HOMEWORK

Anonymity is a double-edged sword. While it is key to honest, helpful feedback, it is an avenue for the chronically dissatisfied person to unleash on the innocent. Some people take great pride in their scathing reviews and see themselves as the Simon Cowell of the interwebs.

All the social media experts advise that businesses respond to online reviews immediately. And this is certainly true for valid complaints. The way a company handles complaints online can turn a bad meal around and make a restaurant seem like Granny spoiling her favorite grandchild. They can become heroes.

If you do receive a negative, anonymous comment online, check to see who wrote the post. If you feel you may be getting trolled, leave one response, and make it a generic one, repeating whatever company policy is appropriate. For instance:

"Thank you for bringing your concern to our attention. We take all comments seriously and investigate all complaints. Our company policy is to serve every customer in a respectful and healthy manner."

Do not engage further. These people just love starting fires and want you to respond over and over in defense of yourself, increasing negative traffic.

I'm sure there are some business owners (and Cruise Directors) who don't read any comments or certainly don't read negative comments, and I think they're missing a golden opportunity.

To quote Bill Gates one more time, "Your most unhappy customers are your greatest source of learning." To be able to listen to your unhappiest customers, you can't put up a defensive wall. And if there's a running theme, week after week after week, then you have to address those issues.

SHIP TO SHORE

Facing criticism is something we can all identify with and probably get better at handling. Here are a few tips:

- Invite feedback.
- Look for trends.
- Address complaints and concerns as soon as possible.
- If you do get negative comments by an anonymous online troll, stay calm and professional. Do not engage. Odds are it is someone in their mother's basement who hasn't had a date since the late 1980s.

EPILOGUE

AND THEN CAME COVID.

In March 2020 the cruise industry and the world shut down. We waited, and we waited, and we waited some more for some sort of return to something. Return to normal? No, the normal we knew and loved would never return. At least how we remembered it.

When the industry initially shut down in the U.S. in March 2020, by order of the Centers for Disease Control and Prevention (CDC), my initial thought was we'd be back sailing by July 2020 at the latest, when I was scheduled to join a ship in Alaska. Oh, silly me. Six months, nine months, a full year went by. Tens of thousands of jobs were lost overnight, not just in the cruise industry, but by those businesses that support the industry: airlines, hotels, restaurants, vendors, suppliers, taxi drivers, luggage handlers, mom and pop souvenir stores, etc. A few ships started sailing in Europe and Asia in late summer 2020 with reduced capacity and very strict protocols and guidelines, and they were quite successful. We were hopeful. Of course there were a few hiccups, but they were handled swiftly and important lessons were learned.

The cruise industry has always been at the forefront of health and safety standards, although you'd never know it by watching cable news. The industry was years ahead of COVID protocols, with hand washing and hand sanitizers placed around the ship. Increased cleaning and sanitizing were a constant. I will put the cleanliness of any shipboard restaurant galley sailing out of the U.S. up against any land-based restaurant. The comparison is not even close. The galleys on board the ships I have worked on have been spotless, and on some ships, galley tours for the guests happened every cruise, so you know they had to be immaculate. When was the last time you were invited into the kitchen of a land-based restaurant? I rest my case.

In the past few years, in order to be as healthy and safe as possible, passengers and crew had to fill out medical questionnaires before they ever boarded the ship, in order to keep the common cold or flu from joining us on board. We expected honest answers, but sometimes people were not forthcoming. With thousands of passengers of all ages joining us every week, coming from some very cold and snowy climates, onto an air-conditioned ship and then out to hot tropical islands, illnesses were bound to break out. A cruise ship is a microcosm of society so of course some people get sick. But the industry does a fantastic job making sure to minimize the spread. Statistics clearly show your chance of getting a common cold or flu on a cruise ship is much less than getting sick on land. And while some cable news networks try hard to show otherwise, the industry is to be commended for their stellar health and safety record.

As soon as COVID hit, the cruise industry sprang into action, working together with doctors, industry leaders, and experts in epidemiology, safety protocols, public health, hospitality, and maritime operations. In September 2020 they produced a sixty-five-plus page report detailing seventy-four best practices to protect the health and safety of passengers and crew, as well as the communities they serve.

The report detailed five key areas:

- Health: Testing, Screening and Exposure Reduction
- Sanitation and Ventilation
- Response, Contingency Planning, and Execution
- Destination and Excursion Planning
- Mitigating Risks for Crew Members

Cruise lines eagerly welcomed the very detailed report and quickly put the recommendations into practice. Again, the cruise industry was leading the way in health and safety protocols.

The COVID-19 vaccine was developed and tested in record time and in late December 2020, the first dose was administered to the general public. We all breathed a little sigh of relief, knowing the end was in sight. But it would take at least nine more months for the majority of the public to get inoculated, and even longer for them to feel completely safe in public and crowded areas. And with the various COVID variants popping up, it will also take time before all ports of call will welcome the cruise ships and their passengers back to their shores.

The thought process for this book began over forty years ago when I joined my first ship, the *T.S.S. Fairwind* for Sitmar Cruises. Little did I know taking my dog for a walk that fateful day in 1976 would lead to the incredible journey I have been blessed to be a part of. But the actual book was written mostly in 2020 and into 2021, when I had a lot more free time on my hands.

And while the cruise industry has not yet fully rebounded, I feel deeply with all my heart it will return stronger and safer than ever, bring new and exciting adventures, and create long-lasting, wonderful memories for generations to come.

I have long said that traveling the world is the absolute best education anyone can receive. The incredible sights, sounds, and smells will live with me forever. Among the highlights of my journey: the extraordinary history found in the various countries and regions I visited (some thousands of years old), the warmth, generosity and compassion of the thousands of people I met along the way, and the stories they shared, even though many times we did not speak the same language. The friends I have made around the world will live in my heart forever.

Traveling the world has certainly served as the foundation of every lesson throughout my career. Create exceptional memories.

Have empathy. Honor others. Respect yourself. Exceed expectations. Communicate. Continually learn. Don't be afraid to make mistakes. Be accountable.

Philosopher Elbert Hubbard once said, "The greatest mistake you can make in life is to be afraid of making one."

Likewise, Will Rogers said, "Good judgment comes from experience, and a lot of that comes from bad judgement."

So, no matter where you are in your life's adventure, take advantage of the opportunities that present themselves to you. Try new things that one day might define your passion. Embrace the journey along the way, because that is where you meet the most fascinating characters. Not everything will turn out as planned, but it could be that crucial next step that ultimately gets you where you want to go. Make those mistakes, but learn from them. Life is way too short, so enjoy this crazy, wild ride.

Because you really can't make this ship up.

I thought my joke was funny, but the audience disagreed.

CONNECT WITH PAUL

I LOOK FORWARD to sailing with you in the near future, and if we don't meet on the high seas, then maybe we'll meet at a conference or a company outing. I would love to speak to your company or association, where we can talk about leadership, management, employee engagement, hospitality, and the wonderful world of cruising.

In the meantime, I would love to stay in touch. You can reach me at:

- www.PaulRutterSpeaks.com (where you can download a free customer service strategy eBook)
- www.LinkedIn.com/in/parutter
- www.Facebook.com/PaulRutterSpeaks
- www.Instagram.com/PaulRutterSpeaks
- www.YouTube.com/PaulRutterSpeaks
- www.Twitter.com/RealPaulRutter
- Email: Paul@PaulRutterSpeaks.com

And make sure to check out our book page with many photographs throughout my career at www.YouCantMakeThisShipUp.com

Let's cruise!

ACKNOWLEDGMENTS

SPECIAL THANKS TO FORMER, fellow Cruise Director Warren Allen Melhuish, who came up with the name for this book. He gave me permission to use it if I gave him credit. Here's full credit to Warren, who is enjoying retirement up in Canada.

Special thanks to Whitney McDuff, Maggie Mills, Kristin Davis and Stacey Crew for their wisdom and guidance with the writing of this book. I couldn't have done it without you.

And special thanks to my wonderful wife of twenty-six years (as of this writing), Jan Downs Rutter. Your help with this book has been invaluable. We met while we both were working on board *Sovereign of the Seas*, proving that shipboard romances do work! While being apart for months at a time is not a recipe for success in many marriages, it has certainly worked for us!

Lightning Source UK Ltd.
Milton Keynes UK
UKHW040853081221
395269UK00003B/887